JOHN AND SALLY McKENNA'S **Bridgestone 100 Best Guides** give all the information you need to enjoy the best of Ireland.These restaurants are chosen for their creativity and excellence, their individuality and ambition, each earning the right to call themselves one of the 100 Best.

The **Bridgestone 100 Best Guides** to Ireland are the most up-to-the-minute guides you can buy. Intensively and dedicatedly researched, with a wealth of detail and description of the chosen entries and written with humour and personal experience, these are the essential travelling companions. If you wish to find the very best of Ireland, you need to travel with John and Sally McKenna's Bridgestone Guides.

READERS' PRAISE FOR THE BRIDGESTONE GUIDES:

"Informative, extremely well written and, above all, accurate... I just wish there was something similar for England, Wales and Scotland".

Mr. D.P., Thaxted

"An excellent, entertaining and necessary guide for anyone hoping to find good food in this country".

Mr. J. K., Crawley

"Your guidebook is a really good one because it does not mislead the reader but offers true and good advice. All the places we tried were all that your guide promised".

Dr. C. B., Malta

"Without your knowledge and book we should not have had such a glorious holiday".

Mrs. B. M., Athy

"Your recommendations were outstanding... we can't wait to try more next year"

L. & M. G., Tallahassee

"We used your excellent guide for a tour of Ireland and found it invaluable...we shall certainly use the guide on our next visit".

N. & S. G. Bayswater

"Wonderfully, wonderfully helpful..."

K.R., Portsmouth

THE BRIDGESTONE 100 BEST RESTAURANTS IN IRELAND 1997/98

FIRST PUBLISHED IN 1997 BY ESTRAGON PRESS, DURRUS,

COUNTY CORK

ISBN 1 874076 22 7

DESIGNED BY NICK CANN

COVER PHOTO BY MIKE O'TOOLE

FOOD STYLING BY JOHN COOKE

PRINTED BY COLOUR BOOKS LTD

■ Whilst every effort has been made to ensure that the information given in this book is accurate, the publishers and authors do not accept responsibility for any errors or omissions or for any change in the circumstances of any of the entries.

THE BRIDGESTONE

100 BEST

RESTAURANTS IN IRELAND 97-98

JOHN & SALLY McKENNA

FOR EDDIE AND RENA

WITH THANKS TO:

Des Collins, Colm Conyngham, Eddie, Nick Cann, Pat Young, Caroline McGrath, Colette Tobin, Mike O'Toole, John Cooke, Paula, Kevin and Ana, Margie Deverell, Jane Weston and Leanna McMichael, Lelia McKenna, Anne Black

JOHN McKENNA was born in Belfast and educated there and in Dublin, where he practised as a barrister before turning to writing in 1989. He has won three Glenfiddich Awards, as Regional Writer, Radio Broadcaster and Restaurant Writer, in 1993, 1994 and 1995.

SALLY McKENNA was born in Kenya, and brought up on the Pacific island of Fiji before coming to Ireland in 1982. She cooked professionally before turning to writing about cookery and food.

John and Sally live in Cork with their children, Connie and Sam.

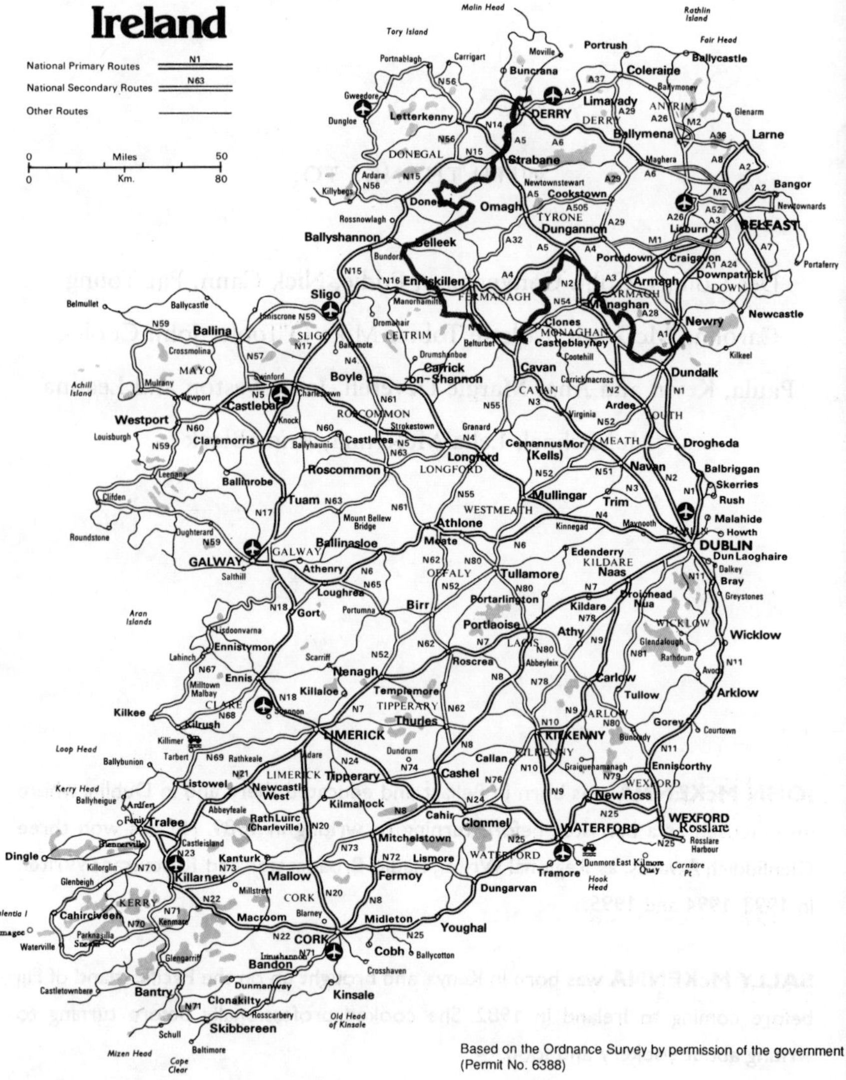

Based on the Ordnance Survey by permission of the government (Permit No. 6388)

CONTENTS

HOW TO USE THIS BOOK

The Bridgestone 100 Best Restaurants in Ireland is arranged **ALPHABETICALLY**, by county, so it begins with County Carlow, which is followed by County Cavan, and so on.

■ Within the counties, the entries are once again listed alphabetically, so Adele's, in Schull, West Cork, is followed by Aherne's, in Youghal, East Cork.

■ Entries in Northern Ireland are itemised together, at the end of the book.

■ The contents of the Bridgestone 100 Best Guide are exclusively the result of the authors' deliberations. All meals and accommodation were paid for and any offers of discounts or gifts were refused.

■ In a number of cases, where we have encountered a restaurateur or hotelier whose work represents a special and unique effort in terms of Irish hospitality, we have awarded these people a star and marked these entries thus: ✪ These people are, simply, the very best at what they do.

■ In other cases where we felt the food was of special interest we have marked the entry with a ⊖, meaning that the entry is worthy of making a special detour to enjoy the hospitality

■ Many of the Country Houses and B&Bs featured in this book are only open during the summer season, which means that they can be closed for any given length of time between October and March. Many others change their opening times during the winter.

PRICES All prices and details are correct at the time of going to press. Should the circumstances of any of the entries change, however, we are unable to accept any responsibility.

■ Finally, we greatly appreciate receiving reports, suggestions and criticisms from readers, and would like to thank those who have written in the past, whose opinions are of enormous assistance to us when considering which 100 places finally make it into this book.

BRIDGESTONE

BRIDGESTONE is the world's largest tyre and rubber manufacturer.

■ Founded in Japan in 1931, it currently employs over 95,000 people in Europe, Asia and America and its products are sold in more than 150 countries. Its European plants are situated in France, Spain and Italy.

■ Bridgestone manufacture tyres for a wide variety of vehicles from passenger cars and motorcycles, trucks and buses to giant earthmovers and aircraft.

■ Many Japanese cars sold in Ireland have been fitted with Bridgestone tyres during manufacture and a host of exotic sports cars including Ferrari, Lamborghini, Porsche and Jaguar are fitted with Bridgestone performance tyres as original equipment.

■ Bridgestone commercial vehicle tyres enjoy a worldwide reputation for superior cost per kilometre performance and its aircraft tyres are used by more than 100 airlines.

■ In 1988 Bridgestone acquired the Firestone Tyre and Rubber Company combining the resources of both companies under one umbrella. This coupled with an intensive research and development programme has enabled Bridgestone to remain the world's most technologically advanced tyre company with testing centres in Japan, USA, Mexico and Italy.

■ Bridgestone tyres are distributed in Ireland by Bridgestone/Firestone Ireland Limited, a subsidiary of the multinational Bridgestone Corporation. A wide range of tyres are stocked in its central warehouse and staff provide sales, technical and delivery services all over the country.

■ Bridgestone tyres are available from tyre dealers throughout Ireland.

For further information:

BRIDGESTONE/FIRESTONE
IRELAND LTD
Unit 4
Leopardstown Office Park,
Dublin 18
Tel: (01) 295 2844
Fax: (01) 295 2858

34 Hillsborough Road,
Lisburn
BT28 1AQ
Tel: (01 846) 678331
Fax: (01 846) 673235

✪ BRIDGESTONE AWARD - THE VERY BEST

➔ WORTHY OF A DETOUR

BRIDGESTONE AWARDS

Co Cork

- ✪ Assolas Country House, Kanturk
- ✪ The Ivory Tower, Cork
- ✪ Longueville House, Mallow
- ✪ The Oystercatcher, Oysterhaven

Co Dublin

- ✪ L'Ecrivain, Dublin
- ✪ Peacock Alley, Dublin
- ✪ Thornton's, Dublin

Co Galway

- ✪ Drimcong House, Moycullen
- ✪ Erriseaske House Hotel, Ballyconeely

Co Kilkenny

- ✪ Lacken House, Kilkenny

Co Sligo

- ✪ Truffles, Sligo

NORTHERN IRELAND

- ✪ Roscoff, Belfast, Co Antrim
- ✪ Shanks, Bangor, Co Down

DETOURS

Co Cavan

- ➔ MacNean Bistro, Blacklion

Co Clare

- ➔ MacCloskey's, Bunratty

Co Cork

- ➔ Lettercollum House, Timoleague
- ➔ Liss Ard Lake Lodge, Skibbereen
- ➔ Island Cottage, Heir Island

Co Dublin

- ➔ Elephant & Castle, Dublin

Co Kerry

- ➔ Allo's Bistro, Listowel
- ➔ Packies, Kenmare

Co Wicklow

- ➔ Avoca Handweavers, Kilmacanogue

NORTHERN IRELAND

- ➔ Nick's Warehouse, Belfast, Co Antrim
- ➔ Sun Kee, Belfast, Co Antrim

INTRODUCTION

Whenever our selection of the 100 best restaurants in Ireland appears, it inevitably provokes a great deal of tut-tutting amongst the old stagers in the restaurant business.

The people to whom we give our awards are always different than those who collect gongs from the bourgeois guides. We leave out places which other critics praise, and we include restaurants and cooks whom others disregard.

Why do we do this? Quite simply, our work differs from other guides because we have a different vision of what makes a good restaurant. We do not award points simply because someone has spent a great deal of money on a place. In fact, we largely disregard the most bourgeois restaurants in the country, simply because it seems to us that a restaurant in which only super-rich people can afford to eat is a stupid idea from the start.

We like restaurants which are accessible to all, and which are characterised by the personalities of the people who run them. We like ambitious, innovative cooking, and if we find it, then a restaurant is included. It doesn't matter if you can't book a table. It doesn't matter if the waiting staff wear t-shirts and the decor is shoestring. All that counts is that the food is as good as it can be, the service is charming, and the atmosphere enjoyable.

That is what we look for, because we believe it is what most people want from a restaurant. It is certainly what we ourselves want when we eat out. This book describes 100 of those cooks and those places, the 100 best.

JOHN AND SALLY McKENNA
DURRUS, COUNTY CORK

THE LORD BAGENAL

James Kehoe
Leighlinbridge, Co Carlow
Tel: (0503) 21668 Fax: 21778

Head Chef: James Kehoe

The wine list in James Kehoe's Lord Bagenal Inn, which may be the restaurant's greatest claim to fame, is a magnificent piece of work, a tender exposition of great wines described in splendidly common-sense language.

"First and foremost, wine is made to be enjoyed" writes Mr Kehoe, the mastermind proprietor behind the list. "If we follow the traditionalists, we will not drink white wine with red meat, nor rosé with fish. I say you drink what you like, and that is what is important, what you like".

This is what is important about Mr Kehoe's splendid wine list, and his fine restaurant. The list is not a bland recital of vintages and varietals, but is instead a careful canvas of fine wines, with the essentials of pleasure and accessibility underpining the reason why each bottle is on the list.

Truth be told, the greatest of Mr Kehoe's achievements is not just his wine list, but the fact that such a spiffing piece of work is put to play in the friendly, sociable and enjoyable bar and restaurant which is The Lord Bagenal Inn.

They play classical music, hang splendid paintings by Irish artists on the walls, have a play area for children, use linen table-cloths and good big glasses, but none of this is the slightest bit arch or reserved.

The pleasure principle is what makes this place special, that and the fact that the enthusiasms which made Mr Kehoe go into the restaurant business when he was fifteen years old have never dimmed.

So, do make a feature of enjoying different wines with the food, for here is cooking whose simplicity means that it marries perfectly with fine wine.

So, begin with a glass of good sherry with some Parma ham to start a meal, and choose perhaps some Sauvignon Blanc as a partner for crab meat in filo pastry. Choosing a good bottle to match with some lemon sole, or baked cod florentine, is pure delight. When game is in season, it is time to turn to the big, long-range reds.

The wines and the food were made for each other and, in the happy embrace of the dining room in The Lord Bagenal, one will be smitten by the delights of this caring, sharing, quaffing place.

■ **OPEN:**
12.30pm-2.15pm Mon-Sun
6pm-10.30pm Mon-Sat. 6pm-9pm Sun

■ **AVERAGE PRICE:**
Lunch £5-£10.50
Dinner from £16
House Wine from £9.95

■ **CREDIT CARDS:**
Visa, Access/Master, Diners

■ **NOTES:**
Full Licence
Wheelchair Access (happy to help)
Children – welcome
High chair, crèche, play area, special menu
The Lord Bagenal Inn is signposted from the N9 Dublin/Carlow/Waterford road, a few miles south of Carlow town.

DANETTE'S FEAST

Danette O'Connell
& David Milne
Urglin Glebe
Bennekerry Carlow
Co Carlow
Tel: (0503) 40817 Fax: 40817

Head Chef: Danette O'Connell

"It's a little treasure".

This was how a friend described Danette O'Connell's restaurant, set in a farmhouse, just outside Carlow town.

The elements to treasure are many and diverse: the fire blazing in the drawing room as you sip aperitifs and nibble on olives and peruse the menus, the truly informed music which plays as you peruse – it may be something as hip as Gavin Bryar's "Farewell to Philosophy" – the eclectic mix of paintings and books, the calm grace of the atmosphere.

But, once embedded in the choice of food, it is farewell to philosophy and hello to deliciousness. Ms O'Connell is an original, inventive cook, marrying a deft technique with a love of rich flavours.

She sets these flavours to play in every direction. Breads, for example, will be flavoured with olives, or with tomato and fennel, perhaps even with pecan nuts and garlic. There is a great fondness for the counter-pointing of tastes also: a smoked chicken salad will come with guacamole and a lemon dressing. A chilli relleno will be filled with Parma ham, goat's cheese and a clever purée of sun dried tomatoes, a successful touch. She will mix pesto with ricotta and tie it up in a filo bundle.

This is smart cooking, designed to impress and assail the taste buds into anticipation. But even when she relaxes into something more simple – like smoked salmon – she will marinate the cucumbers which accompany it and mix crème fraîche with a scallion sauce, again to offer another arrest for the mouth.

Like the musician she is, Danette will allow one a moment of release – a fine bowl of parsnip soup with the tangy zap of the garden – before the tension of good tastes arrives again: chicken breast stuffed with roasted peppers, emmenthal and coriander, with a tomato and soured cream sauce; tender fillet of pork with an apricot, pinenut and tarragon stuffing and with slices of orange skewered with rosemary twigs in a mustard sauce; superb haddock fillets with Dublin Bay prawns and a lemon butter sauce.

Desserts are terrific: sinful chocolate truffle cake with a pecan praline; lovely caramelised lemon tart; terrific crème brûlée with a pear poached in brandy and amaretto.

A little treasure, indeed.

■ OPEN:
7pm-9.30pm Wed-Sat, 1pm-2.30pm Sun

■ AVERAGE PRICE:
Lunch £16.50. Dinner from £24
House Wine from £10

■ CREDIT CARDS:
Visa, Access/Master

■ NOTES:
Wine Licence
Wheelchair Access (1 step to door)
Children – welcome
Leave Carlow on the Hacketstown Road, 2 miles turn left after the Burma Station.

MACNEAN BISTRO ➔

Neven, Joe & Vera Maguire
Blacklion, Co Cavan
Tel: (072) 53022 Fax: 53404

Head Chef: Neven Maguire

Neven Maguire's passion is for the wealth and quality of local foods which he finds round and about him in Cavan.

Ask him why he stays in Blacklion – Blacklion is, truth be told, sort of nowhere, and Mr. Maguire could hold down a job in any kitchen, anywhere – and he immediately replies, "Produce is the backbone of my cooking, and around here I have the best produce".

This trust sets the template for cooking which is simple, inasmuch as it concentrates on a principal ingredient of superb quality, and coaxes the very best out of it.

The memory of a series of dishes from one dinner – a delicate, juicy seafood sausage; a magnificent salad of Eden organic greens; a tenderly stuffed courgette flower filled with a chicken and pesto mousse; a staggering main course of steamed monkfish with a smoked salmon brandade, matched with an essence of lobster and saffron – is the memory of balance and trueness in the cooking, the way in which the ingredients never lost sight of their intrinsic flavours.

For a young man, this is very confident, mature cookery. It showcases ingredients, and the chef's skill, rather than the chef's ego. It takes some chefs years to learn this, but Mr Maguire knows it instinctively.

If he could do no more than cook sweet things, then Neven Maguire would be assured of fame. His dessert cookery is mesmeric, plates such as his chocolate assiette with its busy collection of tuiles, sorbets, langue de chats and chocolate pyramids swirling with the intense energy of a Miro painting.

The counterpoint to such skill lies in the style of the bistro itself, which is decidedly unvogueish. Mr. Maguire's parents, Joe and Vera, opened the MacNean as long ago as 1969, and Mrs Maguire still cooks alongside her son. Out front, the family theme continues, with Neven's sister Naomi masterminding the dining room, her ready response to every enquiry and request a steadfast "Sure, no problem at all".

"No problem at all" could be the motto of the Maguire family. They are a skilful, astute bunch, and they run a restaurant where service and satisfaction are their aim, and their achievement, creating happiness in the local community.

■ OPEN:
6pm-9pm Tue-Sun
Winter closed Mon-Wed
1pm & 3.15pm Sun

■ AVERAGE PRICE:
Sun Lunch £12. Dinner from £22
House Wine from £8.50

■ CREDIT CARDS:
Visa, Access/Master

■ NOTES:
Wine Licence
No Wheelchair Access
Recommended for Vegetarians, special menu £16.95
Children – welcome, high chair, half portions
On the main street.

BARRTRÁ SEAFOOD RESTAURANT

Paul & Theresa O'Brien
Barrtrá, Lahinch, Co Clare
Tel: (065) 81280

Chef: Theresa O'Brien

You overlook the still blueness of Liscannor Bay when sitting in this sweet little restaurant, little more than a couple of commercialised rooms in an otherwise cosy domestic home. And this is one of Paul O'Brien's secrets.

"Will you have lobster tonight?" asks a woman, back in the area on her holidays, and back reserving a table for dinner. It is impossible to say, of course, because no one may have gone out fishing today. Only later, seeing a lone, little red boat making its choppy way into Liscannor Bay, will Paul know that someone has actually gone out. So, yes, there will be lobster tonight.

Not only will there be lobster, but we must tell a story about how Mr O'Brien sometimes gets it. One afternoon, down on the bay, the boat couldn't actually get the bag of lobsters thrown all the way to the shore.

To retrieve them, Paul O'Brien dived in, swam to the bag, and hauled it ashore.

This is a true story.

It is this sort of thing which makes the Barrtrá well nigh irresistible.

Paul does front of house, Theresa cooks, and at busy times their girls lend a hand and put together the desserts. If there is a classic summertime restaurant, with all the holiday-time clichés – friendly food, good service, fine wines, the romance of looking out at the sea as the sun sets – then this is it.

Of course, like any dream, it is founded in the rock-solid realities of hard work. Theresa O'Brien's cooking likes to trade on the classics of the area: turbot with sun-dried tomatoes and olive oil; grilled skate with chives; Burren lamb with thyme; hot buttered lobster, but she also enjoys some nimble experiments, like steamed clams with Thai sauce, or john dory with a spinach pesto.

The vegetables are grown organically, the wine list has gotten better every year and is now a terrific selection culled from all over the world, with excellent bubblies and dessert wines and a good range of half bottles.

This is the sort of little restaurant you dream of stumbling across when on holiday, a personable little oasis of joy and cheering, considerate cooking.

■ **OPEN:**
12.30pm-2pm Tue-Sat, 6pm-10pm Mon-Sat

■ **AVERAGE PRICE:**
Lunch from £2. Dinner from £21
House Wine from £9

■ **CREDIT CARDS:**
Visa, Access/Master, Amex, Diners

■ **NOTES:**
Reservations recommended, by day or night
Wine Licence
Wheelchair Access but not to toilets
Recommended for Vegetarians
Children – well behaved children only, welcome early evening, high chair.
From Lahinch take Miltown Malbray road for 2 miles. Turn right, the restaurant is signposted.

FLAPPERS

Patricia Cahill & Jim McInerney
Main Street, Tulla, Co Clare
Tel: (065) 35711

Head Chef: Patricia Cahill

Patricia Cahill is a quintessential modern Irish cook. Her cooking incorporates many diverse elements, and boasts a cracking sense of ambition. She used to cook in Caherbolane Farmhouse, near to Corofin, helped by her sister Anne and her Mum, Brid.

Ms Cahill could have continued working in Caherbolane, cooking for the guests of the B&B, but if you thought she was going to stay put, you reckoned without that ambition. For Patricia Cahill has made the leap from a small, domestic kitchen in a house, to a fully-fledged, lunch and dinner, wine licensed restaurant. Flappers is in Tulla, near to Ennis, and in it she has fashioned a smart room out of a simple space, decorated with some terrific paintings by Ger Sweeney.

The confidence and stylishness of this woman's cooking has been brought intact to Tulla. Starters such as wild mushroom, cheese and leek tartlets; spicy crab cakes with chilli mayonnaise; and fettucini with a gorgonzola cream sauce and toasted nuts, enjoy a diversity and accuracy of flavours which wins you over. They may range across the globe for influences, but they are never allowed off the leash which binds them to rich, beautifully achieved tastes.

This is succulent cooking, with nothing lost in terms of flavour by the jump into the professional arena, and main courses again show a cook who can wear a chef's toque and a mother's apron at the same time.

Roast rack of lamb au poivre with flageolet beans is absolutely spot on, the meat sweet, the beans soft and comforting. Roast duck breast with a honey Sauternes sauce and a pineapple chutney is pure drool territory, the chutney offsetting the richness of the meat, with the sureness of the skill exemplified by a dish of curried monkfish with an apple and date compote, spiced and sauced to perfection.

If starters and main courses roam around the globe for influences, then desserts bring it all back home: apple tart with hazelnut praline and orange custard is a kiddysome treat, chocolate grand marnier mousse was unapologetically rich and lush

There are great tastes to be enjoyed in Patricia Cahill's cooking, a marvellous confidence and grasp of global influences, but perhaps the nicest thing about her work is the sweet taste of ambition.

■ **OPEN:**
Noon-3pm Mon-Sat
6.30pm-9.45pm Tue-Sat
■ **AVERAGE PRICE:**
Lunch £5.50
Dinner £15
House Wine from £8.90
■ **CREDIT CARDS:**
Visa, Access/Master

■ **NOTES:**
Wine Licence
Wheelchair Access
Children – welcome, high chair
On the Main street in Tulla, across from the Courthouse.

MacCLOSKEY'S ➜

Shaun & Eileen Smith-Roberts
Bunratty House Mews
Bunratty, Co Clare
Tel: (061) 364082 Fax: 364350

Head Chef: Shaun Smith-Roberts

If Shaun Smith-Roberts has one gift which shines out from a panoply of culinary talents, it is his instinct for flavour.

Technically, he works in that modern vein which assembles a variety of ingredients and influences on a plate, and hopes to create an alchemical mix with them.

Smith-Roberts can do this, with aplomb – the dot of sour cream dressing arrayed around a humourously named meatloaf of monkfish and salmon and its clever salad of broccoli with pine nuts; the dynamic and powerful garlic perfume in a dish of white beans with Cratloe lamb – are signs of a cook who has the modern idiom tapped. Impressive, for sure, but what is best about his work is the powerful flavours he harnesses in each invention.

The meatloaf of fish, for example, is so vibrantly fresh that you are lost in admiration for the skill that could make it just so fine, so spot on. The sweetness and juiciness of the lamb, and its perfect counterpoint in some colcannon, could not be bettered. This is great cooking, memorably and deliciously achieved.

He doesn't neglect the essential details which are so integral a part of his quest for perfection: breads are crisply effete, a simple dessert like crème brûlée with pistachio biscuits offers a statement of the very art of sweet things.

His work perfectly resolves the balance between ingredients – soused cucumber with wild Clare smoked salmon; a shallot dressing with oysters; a tongue-tingling spoom scented with geranium; lovely flowerpot bread to partner cauliflower soup; fresh garden feves with a fricassee of monkfish and mussels; a berry compote with freshly churned ice cream – and he guides each thing unerringly home.

Meantime, out front, Eileen Smith-Roberts does the work of three people, meeting, greeting, chatting, and the lovely warren of basement rooms which comprises the restaurant in MacCloskey's are demure, charm-ingly romantic, making this a great date restaurant.

The wine list is excellent, the cheese board one of the country's best, and here is a genuinely exciting restaurant. Don't overlook Bunratty because you associate it with touristic nonsense: MacCloskey's is the real thing.

■ OPEN:
7pm-9.30pm Tue-Sat
■ AVERAGE PRICE:
Dinner £26
House Wine from £10.15
■ CREDIT CARDS:
Visa, Access/Master, Amex, Diners

■ NOTES:
Special Restaurant Licence
No Wheelchair Access
Children – welcome
In Bunratty village, behind the Folk Park. Facing the Shamrock hotel, turn left up Hill Road, travel 20-25 metres through gates to MacCloskey's sign.

MR EAMON'S RESTAURANT

Eamon & Rita Vaughan
Kettle Street
Lahinch, Co Clare
Tel: (065) 81050 Fax: 81810

Head Chef: Eamon Vaughan

Some people's professionalism is so implicit and polished that it gladdens the heart. So it is with the professionalism of Eamon and Rita Walsh.

He cooks with precision and an obvious love of his work.

She serves with a decisive skill which makes her work seem choreographed.

In combination, they make Mr Eamon's a smashing restaurant, someplace that gladdens the heart.

This is wonderful, of course, but what is even more important is the fact that they exhibit this professionalism in Lahinch. This is a busy little town, packed predominantly with golfers who smash it over the celebrated links, and also with holidaymakers and tourists during the season.

To explain the sort of place it is: we once tried to buy a pair of trousers here, and the only – the only – type we could buy were golf trousers. Nothing else. Nothing.

This means, of course, that the Vaughans could sit back and cash in, by doing soulless food for folk in golf slacks who won't, most likely, ever come back to the town.

But they don't do this. In Mr Eamon's, every customer is treated with respect, and every dish is treated likewise.

The selection of starters is a list of classics – grilled St. Tola cheese with sesame seeds; Caesar salad; a filo pastry parcel of prawns and cream cheese with a tomato and basil sauce, and something clever like calf's tongue with a tomato chutney will be deliciously rendered.

The emphasis of the main courses is based on fish – fillet of turbot with a lovely sauce soubise; Aran scallops with a vermouth sauce; hot buttered lobster – with meat dishes sticking with classics such as sirloin with a pepper and mushroom sauce or duckling with an orange sauce. Timeless dishes which receive classic treatment, all the way through to nursery food finishers like bread and butter pudding, or ice cream with butterscotch sauce.

The room itself is agreeably informal, and overall one is struck by the very generosity of everything about this restaurant – the patience of the service, the attention to detail, the value for money, the respect for their work which the owners and staff exhibit with every little thing they do.

■ OPEN:
7pm-9.30pm Mon-Sun
Open six days mid season
Closed mid Jan-mid Mar

■ AVERAGE PRICE:
Dinner £22
House Wine £9.50

■ CREDIT CARDS:
Visa, Access/Master, Amex, Diners

■ NOTES:
Wine Licence
Full Wheelchair Access
Children – well behaved children only, High chair
Situated in Lahinch village.

SHEEDY'S SPA VIEW HOTEL

Frank & Patsy Sheedy
Lisdoonvarna
Co Clare
Tel: (065) 74026 Fax: 74555

Head Chef: Frankie Sheedy

Let us be perfectly honest about Lisdoon.

Its glory days are behind it. Its worldwide fame, which is due mainly to the annual matchmaking competition, is undeserved. It has some nice little places, but is otherwise a resort town in need of serious re-invention.

It is, truth be told, a little bit sad.

Now, let us be perfectly honest about Sheedy's.

It is a modest resort hotel, well run by good staff who know their job, but in The Orchid it boasts a serious restaurant, with real cooking, and true ambition.

If there is one thing which should change your mind, and actually bring you to Lisdoon, then it is Frankie Sheedy's cooking.

Here is a creative cook, one evening serving the amazing Burren lamb with a garlic jus, another time confecting it with a courgette and tomato gateau and changing the sauce to a rosemary and thyme jus.

He might serve an escalope of salmon with a sage and walnut pesto, or maybe just treat it simply and place the fish on a bed of spinach with a light saffron sauce.

This is imaginative, real cooking, all the way from a pheasant terrine, or perhaps a tian of fresh crab, to start, onto a smoked haddock bisque or a crisp salad, then maybe some monkfish with melted leeks and apple, or the indulgence of their speciality, lobster served either plain, or with garlic butter.

Desserts are similarly ambitious: iced lemon curd and lemon ice cream tart with an orange and dark chocolate sauce; a Bailey's and pear cheese cake, or chocolate gateau with a coffee bean and strawberry coulis.

Prices are excellent, but one would like to see a little more effort put into the wine list, which is fairly predictable and which would benefit from the involvement of more suppliers. The cooking deserves something more unpredictable than this assortment. Service is excellent, correctly paced, appositely judged to suit the relaxed style of the hotel.

So remember. The best match-making done in Lisdoon is the culinary pairings brought together on Frankie Sheedy's dinner plates.

And you will be happy ever after.

■ **OPEN:**
6.30pm-8.45pm Mon-Sun (closed Oct-Apr)
■ **AVERAGE PRICE:**
Lunch from £12.50
Dinner from £21.50
House Wine £9.50
■ **CREDIT CARDS:**
Visa, Access/Master, Amex, Diners

■ **NOTES:**
Open lunch, but booking essential
Full Pub Licence
Wheelchair Access apart from one step at front door
Children – welcome, high chair, special menus
I mile of the N68, on the second road to village.

AHERNE'S SEAFOOD RESTAURANT

The Fitzgibbon Family
163 North Main Street
Youghal, Co Cork
Tel: (024) 92424 Fax: 93633
e-mail: ahe@iol.ie

Head Chef: David Fitzgibbon

Aherne's is one of those restaurants which can, on occasion, not merely do things well, but do them definitively. So, the following story is true.

A man, who happens to make his living writing about food, visited Aherne's Seafood Bar for lunch, one April day, in the course of a gastronomic trip to Ireland. He ordered, for a main course, some cod.

After his lunch, he talked about the cod, and its definitive excellence. It was nothing less than perfect, the best type of masterpiece, because it had been achieved from such a simple, almost derided, base.

And, for the remainder of his stay in Ireland, he was happy to tell all, and sundry, about the cod in Aherne's. Masterly. So simple. Perfect.

When he got home he did describe, for his readers, some of the other sights and bites he had enjoyed. But, the centrepiece of the long article he wrote dealt with the cod. So simple. Perfect.

Provoking this sort of reaction amongst its diners has ensured the success of Aherne's in its long history.

The restaurant mixes a formal professionalism with the relaxed nature of a family operation, combining the formality of a softly decorated dining room, with the informality of reliable and extremely enjoyable food served in the front bar.

The food, in both the restaurant and the bar, intelligently searches out the true tastes of the fish around which David Fitzgibbon's cooking is centred. And it is most usually the simple things which are so mightily impressive: a pair of fillets of turbot, dusted with flour and fried, served only with some lemon butter, will be a statement of fine fish cookery.

But if Aherne's is perfect in these ways – and we should mention the service, here, for it is terrific – then there are other areas where they could do with aiming a little higher.

Their vegetable cookery, for example, lacks panache and suitability. Fish cookery demands individual vegetable selections, not a pot luck mix which you receive whether you are having baked cod with a herb crust or chargrilled sirloin steak.

The wine list is good, and fairly priced. The food in the bar, by the way, is excellent, and makes perfect on-the-road food.

■ OPEN:
12.30pm-2pm, 6.30pm-9.30pm Mon-Sun

■ AVERAGE PRICE:
Lunch £15. Dinner from £25
House Wine from £11.50

■ CREDIT CARDS:
Visa, Access/Master, Amex, Diners

■ NOTES:
Full Pub Licence
Full Wheelchair Access
Children – welcome, high chair
On the N25 in the centre of Youghal and well singposted.

ANNIE'S

Dano & Annie Barry
Main Street
Ballydehob
Co Cork
Tel: (028) 37292

Head Chefs: Dano & Annie Barry

Annie Barry has the bestest, nicest, manner of any restaurant owner in the country.

Her pacific nature with kids is legendary – Mrs Barry herself, of course, is too modest to agree with this – but she works her spell on adult kids with the same surreptitious ease, and quickly has you boggle-eyed and goo-goo with anticipation for the treat that is dinner in Annie's.

The restaurant is just a single room with tables in multiples of pairs, nice and bright in summertime if you choose an early evening dinner, and everyone begins with drinks across the road in Levis's pub while you choose from the menu. Indeed, the sight of Annie hopping across the street between restaurant and bar, armed with menus, is one of the great characteristics of the village in summertime.

Mr Barry doesn't try to do too much – and doesn't need to do too much – to coax the very best from his good ingredients. The most preparation a piece of Sally Barnes's super smoked salmon ever needs is a squidge of lemon. He does nice old-fashioned things such as putting sautéed lamb's kidneys on toast, stuffing mussels with garlic and breadcrumbs. Black sole on the bone is announced as "simply grilled". If it ain't broke, they might say, why fix it?

With scallops as big and fat and coral-clawed as the ones you find in here, then a cream and white wine sauce may almost seem superfluous, but the sauce will be generous and precise, as generous and precise as an apricot sauce around a piece of finely roasted duck, or the cider and apple sauce with a fillet of pork. The cooking may be light in execution, but it is deep in savour.

Right down to the very simple things – some luscious boiled spuds which you gobble up with the appetite of someone who has been hacking turf all day long, some baked cod or maybe, the regular's choice, a super-duper steak and some fab chips – Annie's gets it right. Desserts bring things to a rousing climax: hot fudge cake with cream; roasted almonds and Bailey's ice cream, chocolate profiteroles. The temperament of this little place never changes, and never needs to, for who would tamper with a classic?

■ OPEN:
7pm-9.30pm Tue-Sat
■ AVERAGE PRICE:
Dinner from £22
House Wine from £11.50
■ CREDIT CARDS:
Visa, Access/Master

■ NOTES:
Wine Licence
Wheelchair Access but not to toilet
Children – welcome
Ballydehob town centre

NB Dano & Annie run a Coffee shop in the nearby bookshop. Open summer months 10am-6pm Mon-Sat

ARBUTUS LODGE HOTEL

Declan & Patsy Ryan
Middle Glanmire Road
Montenotte, Cork City
Tel: (021) 501237, Fax: 502893
e-mail: arbutus@iol.ie

Head Chef: Kevin Arundel

The grand old dame of Cork cooking sails serenely on, as always under the guidance of Declan Ryan. The essential mainstays of the Arbutus are as fine as ever – the wonderful collection of art, the staggering, award-winning wine list, the golly-gosh views out over the city from the hill of Montenotte, the calm and endearing service which has always been such a welcoming feature. Indeed, these elements have become not just features but fixtures of Cork eating and drinking, so much so that it is almost easy to take them for granted.

The wine list, for example, has long been famous. Judiciously selected, and a model of just how to describe wines by the use of concise, precise, intelligent, well-understood notes, it impresses today because of the constant overhauls which it enjoys, the constant new additions alongside the mainstays of Burgundy and Bordeaux. The Arbutus list is a testament not just to Declan Ryan's obsession with wine, but to his hard work, constantly searching out and selecting new purveyors of vinous excellence.

So the air of changelessness which is the pervasive note of Arbutus is actually something of a lie. There is constant change here, constant attention to new fashions and trends, constant questioning of just what they do.

Whilst the popular conception of Declan Ryan and Kevin Arundel's cooking is that of a distinctly Cork cuisine – spiced beef used with mushrooms in filo; the famous dish of kassler – smoked loin of pork – served with cabbage; Cork cruibins; lovage soup; a tansy sauce to accompany the aromatic drisheen – there have been many innovations to absorb the influences of the Mediterranean in recent times – baked aubergine with roast peppers, West Cork cheese and pesto; confit of duck leg with spinach and figs; pan-fried red mullet with baby leeks and a bouillabaise sauce; escalope of salmon with sun-dried tomatoes and a basil beurre blanc. The scope of the cooking in the restaurant is grand and involved, whilst the informal food served in the bar is imaginative.

■ OPEN:
8am-10am, 1pm-2pm
7pm-9.30pm Mon-Sun

■ AVERAGE PRICE:
Lunch £15.50
Dinner from £23.50
House Wine from £10.15

■ CREDIT CARDS:
Visa, Access/Master, Amex, Diners

■ NOTES:
Full Pub Licence
Wheelchair Access apart from six steps at entrance
Children – well behaved children only, high chair
Just north of the city centre, turn left at McCurtain Street up Summer Hill, then at St Luke's Cross, right to Mdl Glanmire Rd.

ASSOLAS COUNTRY HOUSE ✪

Joe & Hazel Bourke
Kanturk
Co Cork
Tel: (029) 50015
Fax: 50795

Head Chef: Hazel Bourke

"My grandmother would have appreciated Mrs. Bourke's willingness to leave well alone", Maureen Fant wrote in The New York Times, to describe Hazel Bourke's cooking.

Ms Fant went on: "Her style is modern and light but also conservative, a showcase for the fine raw materials... " a precise and accurate pen portrait of a cook who has one of the most distinctive styles of any chef in Ireland.

Perhaps part of the magic of Mrs Bourke's work rests with the fact that she cooks in Assolas, one of the most dreamily romantic houses in the country. The house is grand, and ancient, but exudes the atmosphere of a family home, which it is. The Queen Anne dining room is cosseting red, and cloistered, serene and endlessly suitable for a style of cooking which mesmerises with its simplicity.

Indeed, Hazel Bourke's work is so understated that it can be difficult to understand why she is such a darling of the critics. If we had to put our finger on any one reason – aside from the fact that the food is utterly delicious – it might be the fact that it is so much the expression of a conscientious culinary philosophy, which values the integrity of raw ingredients, and modestly sees the function of the cook as being to unveil their flavours.

Hazel Bourke's ability to coax the natural flavours from food means that each dish offers varied taste sensations, as the food changes and adapts. The knockout roulade of roasted peppers and aubergines which she serves with creamed St. Tola goat's cheese. Kenmare mussels in a brioche case. The lovely loin of lamb, its gravy scented with garden rosemary. Free range chicken stuffed with courgette and cream cheese. A strudel of garden spinach and vegetables. This is food which looks simple on the page, and which is even simpler on the plate. But what is not simple is the rich breadth of taste which all the food enjoys.

Hazel Bourke's cooking is so special that it leads one, ultimately, to conclude that perhaps she is not, in fact, conservative. More likely, this style shows a chef with true daring. Let us go back to Curnonsky: "Cooking? That's when things taste of themselves!". Indeed that is cooking, and Hazel Bourke expresses it better than anyone else.

■ **OPEN:**
7pm-8.30pm Mon-Sun
■ **AVERAGE PRICE:**
Dinner from £30. House Wine from £14
■ **CREDIT CARDS:**
Visa, Access/Master, Amex, Diners

■ **NOTES:**
Non resident booking essential
Full Pub Licence
Wheelchair Access, but not to toilets
Children – over 10 yrs welcome
Take the N72 Mallow/Killarney Road, and 10km west of Mallow you will see the first signpost at a small junction.

BALLYMALOE HOUSE

The Allen Family
Yeats Room Restaurant,
Ballymaloe House, Shanagarry
Midleton, Co Cork
Tel: (021) 652531 Fax: 652021
e-mail: bmaloe@iol.ie

Head Chef: Rory O'Connell

The culinary philosophy of Myrtle Allen's Ballymaloe House is durable, homespun, simple, ageless.

First, a country house hotel must encourage a circle of producers around and about you to produce the best foods they can, and you must support them as best you can. Keep everything local and, thereby, enjoy the benefit of foods which express themselves in terms of the micro-climate in which they are produced and reared. Enjoy their uniqueness, and value this, rather than any vain exclusivity.

Secondly, try to be as self-sufficient as you can: grow your own spuds, make your own chutneys, produce as much of the food you need, through your own endeavours.

Then, when it comes to the cooking of this food, do it from scratch, and do it with ingredients as pristinely fresh as possible. No egotism must blunt the edge of the cooking: you just allow the food to speak of and for itself.

Then, when it comes to serving the food, do it simply, but courteously and as graciously as you can, with easy, spontaneous dialogue between customer, waiting staff and cook, a culinary conversation. Have good paintings in the dining room to lift the spirit, and a spirited ambience throughout the house.

This is a simple modus operandi, a startlingly obvious one, and Myrtle Allen and her team have never lost sight of this creed of simplicity, this respect for plainness in thinking and cooking, in twenty five years. During that time, the philosophy of Ballymaloe has remained consistent: respect for the fruits of the land, air and sea. Respect for the long-held culinary codes which best transform these fruits, codes which are now in the hands of head chef Rory O'Connell. Respect for the person who will enjoy the fruits of the cook's labours and, just as important, respect demanded for the efforts of the cook.

Many people find it difficult to see this simplicity at work. But there are many, still, who see in the Ballymaloe philosophy a logical, conscientious, organic way of working with the world. For them it is this deep thread, just as much as the delicious presentations on a plate which you will remember for years afterwards, which makes Ballymaloe special.

■ **OPEN:**
12.30pm-3pm, 7pm-midnight Mon-Sun

■ **AVERAGE PRICE:**
Lunch £16.50. Dinner from £31.50
House Wine from £13

■ **CREDIT CARDS:**
Visa, Access/Master, Amex, Diners

■ **NOTES:**
Full Pub Licence
No Wheelchair Access
Children – welcome, high chair for children's tea only
2 miles outside Cloyne.

LA BIGOUDENNE

Rodolphe & Noelle Semeria
28 McCurtain Street
Fermoy
Co Cork
Tel: (025) 32832

Rodolphe and Noelle Semeria's La Bigoudenne restaurant is as prototypically French as the ceremonial, luridly-phallic, sharp-pointed hat which gives the restaurant its name.

It is a restaurant which proves that you can take the French out of France, where Monsieur and Madame Semeria hail from, but you can never take the Frenchness, that inimitable je-ne-sais-quoi, out of their cooking. Its element of difference, alone, is one good reason to step in through the doors, off the main street of bustling Fermoy.

During the day it is a simple café, with splendid food that perfectly restores the traveller: filled baguettes, chunky pâtés, home-made soups. A good on-the-road place, just as you would hope to find in France.

The speciality of the restaurant, and one that makes it worth travelling any distance to try, are the crêpes: the savoury ones – filled with ham and egg, egg and cheese, chicken and mushroom with cream, salad and blue cheese; and the sweet ones – filled with stewed apple, chocolate, pear and ice-cream. They are splendid on-the-road food, giving energy, brightening the soul.

At night, La Bigoudenne is transformed. The napery is brought out, and everything changes, with that seamless, easy French poise, to a more formal setting. For dinner, then, perhaps a glass of kir to begin, then a well envisioned dish of veal with some ceps, or fine fresh river trout or, one of their specialities, sweet fresh lobster with butter, maybe even a little chicken curry cooked with pineapple. Desserts are classical – chocolate mousse, tarte tatin – and just right.

The food, the techniques and the styling come straight from northern France, and they create simple, enjoyable, calm tastes, and a confident, almost serene atmosphere.

In this neck of the woods, where there are all-too-few restaurants, La Bigoudenne is a vital asset, a fact which its devoted, faithful – and considerable – clientele attest to.

■ OPEN:
12.30pm-6pm, 7pm-10pm Tue-Sat
7pm-10pm Sun

■ AVERAGE PRICE:
Lunch £4.40-£6
Dinner from £16-£21
House Wine from £9.75

■ CREDIT CARDS:
Visa, Access/Master

■ NOTES:
Wine Licence
Wheelchair Access
Children – welcome, special menu on request
On the main street, which is also the main road between Dublin and Cork, 200 yards before the main traffic lights if you are coming from the Cork direction.

BLAIR'S COVE RESTAURANT

Philippe & Sabine De Mey
Durrus, Bantry
Co Cork
Tel: (027) 61127 Fax: 61127

Head Chef: Sabine De Mey

Dinner in Blair's Cove is centred around twin monuments.

Firstly, there is the monumental selection of hors d'oeuvres, a tiered-table smorgasbord of starters, which is the centrepiece of this stone-walled, elegant, vaulted dining room.

Secondly, there is the monumental wood fire grill, set on a height at the far end of the room, from which the smoky, seductive smell of cooking meats emanates, and which is one of the most seductive features of this venerable restaurant.

You begin by plundering the array of hors d'oeuvres, choosing a selection from amongst smoked herring roe with its crackly flavour, cucumber stuffed with crab meat, fresh boiled prawns, butter-crusted pâtés, maybe some sweet and some sour pickled herrings, maybe a pair of gigas oysters or a slice or two of smoked salmon, maybe some mushrooms in a curry sauce.

And whilst it is the simply-grilled meats which are the centrepiece of main courses, there are other more modern and well-tuned choices written on the blackboard: superb loin of venison served with a venison sausage; confit of duck with 5 spice powder and herbs, slightly under-grilled fillet of tuna cooked perfectly.

But it is to the grilled meats that newcomers must be directed, for on occasion they can be perfect. Indeed, if we speak of restaurants which can achieve things in a definitive fashion, we must include Philippe and Sabine's meat cookery in Blair's Cove. On the right night, you can eat grilled beef or lamb in here which is as fine as you could possibly imagine: fillet of beef with a shallot sour cream, perhaps, superb rib of beef with perfect bearnaise, lamb with its own juices and flageolets.

Finish dinner with a hungry raid to the piano, on top of which lie the great local cheeses from Durrus or Gubbeen, then cap it all with some well-made chocolate mousse, some tiramisu, and it is sublime.

For many people, dinner in Blair's Cove has been one of the most memorable meals of their entire lives, and there is something enigmatically, mysteriously romantic about it all. They can, on occasion, slip from their own high standards, but when this restaurant is on form, it is a mighty establishment.

■ OPEN:
7.30pm-9.30pm Tue-Sat
(open Mon in Jul & Aug)
■ AVERAGE PRICE:
Dinner from £27.50
House Wine from £12
■ CREDIT CARDS:
Visa, Access/Master

■ NOTES:
Restaurant Licence
Wheelchair Access, but not to toilets
Children – welcome, half portions
1.5 miles outside the village of Durrus on the Barleycove/Mizen Head road.
Look for the blue gates on the right hand side.

CASINO HOUSE

Kerrin & Michael Relja
Coolmain Bay, Kilbrittain
Co Cork
Tel: (023) 49944 Fax: 49945

Head Chef: Michael Relja

Casino House may be the sort of pristine and clever place which initially attracts folk who want to admire its cool, pacific style of decoration, and the whacky artworks on the walls – sandblasted kitchen utensils and crockery created by Kerrin Relja's Mum, marvellous pieces which are both funny and intriguing.

But if you come initially to see the knives and forks and plates on the walls, then it will be what you eat with the knives and forks from the plates on the tables which will bring you back. Michael Relja can cook.

He likes very upfront, concentrated tastes, and uses every opportunity to graft another flavour into a dish. Typical of his style is to grill a fine black sole, and then not only dress it with spring onions and accompany it with wild rice, but to finish the dish with a fruity sauce.

This is risk-taking of a high order – get one thing wrong and you end up with a fiasco – but Mr Relja has a cool style to suit the cool interior of Casino House. Whilst the restaurant can seem well-named, with every dish promising some manner of a gamble, Mr Relja is no reckless man with the culinary dice. He brings home the bacon. He is accomplished.

His cooking wears all the notes of modern European fusion cookery, so one will find that he serves his pollo alla diavola with an olive pasta; serves fillet steak with a Burgundy sauce and potato cakes; wraps saddle of lamb in a herb crust and matches it with both aubergines and gnocchi, and will rustle up mousse au chocolat and appletart Alsace to conclude a Sunday lunch.

The restaurant occupies the downstairs of this fine house, set hard by the winding coast road from Kinsale out westwards, but unfortunately the dining room does not take advantage of the marvellous views across Coolmain Bay. One hopes, then, for a sunny Sunday and the chance to eat lunch outside on the terrace, when both the view and this fine cooking can be enjoyed.

Kerrin Relja is a confident young woman, able to mind a batch of kids and a batch of customers at one and the same time. Do look out for some of the unusual German wines on the list – the Ruppertsberger Riesling Kabinett from the Pfalz is a beauty – which match wonderfully well with this food.

■ OPEN:
1pm-9pm Mon-Sun Jul & Aug
7pm-9pm Thur-Tue Apr-Oct
7pm-9pm Fri-Sun, 1pm-3pm Sun Nov-Jan.
Closed Feb-mid Mar.

■ AVERAGE PRICE:
Lunch £4-£12. Dinner from £16
House Wine £9.90

■ CREDIT CARDS:
Visa, Access/Master

■ NOTES:
Wine Licence
Wheelchair Access
Children – welcome, high chair
On the coast road (R600) between Timoleague & Kinsale.

CHEZ YOUEN

Youen Jacob
The Pier
Baltimore
Co Cork
Tel: (028) 20136
Fax: 20495

Head Chef: Youen Jacob

The stories about Youen Jacob's restaurant are legend.

"I came in at noon, one Sunday, after a drink in Bushe's Bar. I left, I think it was about nine thirty, that night".

"I started lunch in here one Sunday at two o'clock, and left that night at ten o'clock".

You hear these stories about Chez Youen, and only half believe them. Cork hyperbole, you reckon. Exaggerated. Expanded. Anything to tell a good story.

So, we must confess that the last time we entered Youen Jacob's lovely restaurant in Baltimore, it was shortly after noon, after a drink in Bushe's Bar.

We had a splendid lunch – the shellfish platter; scallops à la crème; roast lamb, tarte tatin – and we had the wines – Gros Plant; Bordeaux Clairette – and, blow me!, but wasn't it nearly seven o'clock and where on earth has the day gone?

He can do this sort of thing, Youen Jacob, because he loves food, loves cooking, loves the business of sharing his restaurant space with customers, and he is fortunate to enjoy an easy, expert affinity with his craft.

An emulsion of pristine, slurpy mayonnaise in which to dunk your shellfish platter will be just right. A hollandaise of angelic lightness will underpin a fillet of salmon. Cream with green peppercorns for roasted beef will be perfectly judged.

Indeed, with fish and shellfish, it can seem that the sauce is truly the star, the real performer on a stage otherwise set by the fish. It is simple food, classic French food, and it is perfectly done.

Chez Youen has always been someplace special, someplace with a party atmosphere. For many, indeed, it is perhaps the characteristic West Cork restaurant: unusual, slightly crazy, often unforgettable. M Jacob cooks some things as well as they can possibly be cooked – the perfect shellfish, the sweet lamb, the best-you-ever-ate tarte tatin – and these, and the carefree, happy atmosphere, makes Chez Youen a place you always hunger to go back to. Just remember to cancel all appointments, and try to go in the height of the season, when the restaurant is at its best.

■ OPEN:
12.30pm-2.30pm, 6pm-10.30pm Mon-Sun
(closed lunch & Tue off season)

■ AVERAGE PRICE:
Lunch £12.50
Dinner from £21.50
House Wine from £12.50

■ CREDIT CARDS:
Visa, Access/Master, Amex, Diners

■ NOTES:
Wine Licence
Wheelchair Access, but not to toilets
Children – welcome, £5 menu
Overlooking the Harbour in Baltimore.
Follow signs from Skibbereen.

CAFÉ PARADISO

Denis Cotter & Bridget Healy
16 Lancaster Quay
Western Road
Cork
Tel: (021) 277939

Head Chef: Denis Cotter

The magical element of Denis Cotter's work lies not just in the bright wrap of flavours which his cooking summons, but in the fact that his cooking is so complete in itself.

You can eat lunch or dinner in Café Paradiso, the modest room on Cork's Western Road where Mr Cotter and his partner, Bridget Healy, have been squeezing out sparks for the last four years, and find that each dish is perfectly primed to send the flavour buttons in our brains ringing ding-a-ling with delight.

Chilled beetroot soup with cucumber and scallions, zing! Broad beans in basil and lemon, ooh! Sushi of carrot, scallion and rocket with wasabi, pickles and a dipping sauce, wow! Courgette and sweet potato tortilla with avocado salsa and polenta on spiced greens, mama! Potato and rocket cakes with a stew of butterbeans and vegetables with herbs, olives and goat's cheese, phew! Roasted sweet peppers with a caper and pine nut stuffing on wilted chard with a mustard cream, bliss!

Gorgeous food with gameball flavours, served in a room which manages to make you feel as invigorated and, indeed, youthful, as the cooking. You could pay the modest bill and head home happy, and it might be only sometime later that the realisation will strike you. No meat. No fowl. No fish.

Café Paradiso is a vegetarian restaurant, but you might never know it. Its cuisine is a million miles away from the self-denying, meat-substitute style of vegetarian cooking as you can possibly get. Mr Cotter's cooking is, instead, a modern, multi-cultural embrace of styles and ingredients, which he harmonises in expert fashion. Meat is not on the agenda. It doesn't need to be.

Like any good cook, Denis Cotter is endlessly self-critical: "My cooking is now evolving on its own path", he says. "What I do now makes my work years ago seem pubescent and childishly 'inventive'. Well, to me anyway."

He is too hard on himself, of course, but out of this critical acumen has evolved not only the country's best vegetarian restaurant, but a very personal and creative style of cooking, a style which is complete, and logical.

■ OPEN:
10.30am-10.30pm Tue-Sat (lunch served 12.30pm-3pm, dinner 6.30pm-10.30pm)

■ AVERAGE PRICE:
Lunch from £4.50
Dinner from £14-£20
House Wine from £9.40

■ CREDIT CARDS:
Visa, Access/Master

■ NOTES:
Wine Licence
Wheelchair Access, but not to toilets
Children – welcome, high chair, books, toys
Opposite Jury's Hotel on the Western Road.

DUNWORLEY COTTAGE RESTAURANT

Katherine Norén
Butlerstown, Bandon, Co Cork
Tel: (023) 40314

Head Chef: Katherine Norén

In many ways, Dunworley Cottage is a quintessential Bridgestone guide restaurant.

Where is it? Well, the middle of nowhere, sort of, buffeted by sea winds, close to an achingly beautiful coastline.

What is it like? Just a couple of rooms, really, one of them a conservatory. Simply, indeed plainly, decorated, though with nice touches of humour.

Who runs it? Katherine Norén, who hails from Sweden, and who has introduced many elements of Swedish cooking into the menu, perhaps the most noticeable amongst them her native country's love of cured fish.

Why should anyone want to know about a simple little place in the middle of nowhere where you can get cured fish?

For the simple reason that there are tastes to be enjoyed in Dunworley which no one else can create. Mrs Norén loves food, and loves the provocation of cooking and inventing in the kitchen. She has most recently been working with a brilliant young man called Mattias Carlsson – remember the name, you'll likely hear more of this young firebrand – and his skills and Mrs Norén's passion led Dunworley to astonishing culinary heights, with the boss and her chef seeking to outdo one another.

One summer evening dinner produced a mussel soup which had such a voluptuous, sensual texture as to border on the obscene. There was a great salmon salad – minuscule pieces of egg and capers with the fish, and a delicate mussel salad. Main courses of smoked veal loin on a reduction of red wine and port and a fish selection were magnificent. Vegetables bristled with vigour. A chocolate pear drop and an elderflower mousse were sublime. Magnificent.

But perhaps the final reason why Dunworley is a quintessential Bridgestone guide restaurant lies in the fact that its brilliance allows us to invoke a brilliant practitioner in another art form, who hails from Mrs Norén's own country, and lets us make an obscure joke.

Watching Ingmar Bergman's movies rarely fills one with pleasure but, leaving Dunworley after an August dinner, you will surely be smiling the smiles of a summer night.

■ OPEN:
Noon-3pm, from 6.30pm Wed-Sun (check hours both high season and off season)

■ AVERAGE PRICE:
Lunch from £5
Dinner from £21
House Wine from £10.25

■ CREDIT CARDS:
Visa, Access/Master, Amex, Diners

■ NOTES:
Restaurant Licence
Wheelchair Access, but not to toilets
Children – welcome, high chair, £3 menu
The restaurant is signposted from Timoleague.

THE EARL OF ORRERY RESTAURANT

Colm Falvey
140 North Main Street
Youghal
Co Cork
Tel: (024) 93208

Head Chef: Colm Falvey

Colm Falvey's little restaurant is as simple a space as you could find, a classic shoestring operation which extends to just a pair of rooms, fronting onto Main Street, which have been joined together.

There are about seven or eight tables, a few nifty paintings on the wall, a small counter and a kitchen in behind. It is a real Mom 'n' Pop place, an Irish equivalent of a village trattoria or a provincial café, and like those very establishments we value so much in Italy or France, Mr Falvey's restaurant is a simple space where the food has its own personality, its own charm.

Both his method and his style are essentially simple. Whatever fresh fish is landed on the day is described on a slip of paper with other new arrivals, so some squid may be deep fried and paired with a fine, sweet provençal sauce, or a fillet of plaice will be just pan fried in garlic butter.

These dishes augment the basic menus, which offer classic crowd pleasers such as wild salmon with a tomato and fresh herb salsa, or sirloin steak parisienne, or a simple rack of lamb with garden herbs.

His leanings are always towards no-nonsense, adroit dishes: Caesar salad; duck confit with lentils; mushroom and smoked ham pancake.

This sort of cooking is unambiguously flavourful, and Mr Falvey knows exactly how to grab the essence of a dish by the throat.

He never lets complication get in the way of goodness, so some roast loin of pork with fresh herbs, tomato and garlic will be a solid sender of good tastes, full of the comforting, agrestic nature of meat.

Small details, like really careful vegetable cookery, and good gratins and purées, make for truly enjoyable food which shows a lot of care.

The wine list is short but rings the changes through varietals and countries, and there are plenty of choices to suit this smart cooking.

They could maybe make the music a little funkier for night-time, which would make it more in tune with the youthful nature of the cooking, but otherwise the simple, spirited nature of The Earl of Orrery is just right on the money.

■ OPEN:
Noon-3pm, 6pm-10pm Mon-Sun
(Sep-Jun noon-3pm Mon-Sun, 6pm-9.30pm Sun)

■ AVERAGE PRICE:
Lunch £4-£8
Dinner from £14-£20
House Wine from £10.50

■ CREDIT CARDS:
Visa, Access/Master

■ NOTES:
Wine Licence
Full Wheelchair Access
Children – well behaved children for lunch only (no high chairs)
Three quarters of the way through Youghal on the right hand side of the main street, coming from Cork.

THE FARM GATE & THE FARM GATE CAFE

Maróg O'Brien & Kay Harte
Midleton, Co Cork
Tel: (021) 632771
Head Chef: Marog O'Brien

English Market, Cork
Tel: (021) 278134
Head Chef: Glenna O'Reilly

The restaurant revolution which has overhauled Ireland in the last decade has occasionally blinded us to the merits of those restaurateurs who calmly and quietly go about their job, creating valuable places valued by local people, concentrating not on winning stars and banging gongs, but in serving simple food with good cheer and good grace.

It is these folk who are the quintessential professionals, for their reward is not media exposure, but the more fundamental and profound reward of making people happy.

Kay Harte and her sister Maróg O'Brien are quintessential professionals, quintessential restaurateurs. They run the pair of Farm Gates – the long-established restaurant and shop in Midleton, and the newer, upstairs daytime restaurant in the English Market in Cork city, and the keynote of their style is simplicity.

Maróg, who cooks dinner in Midleton on Friday and Saturday nights, will express it thus: "Buy the freshest – then leave it alone.

"I never know what fish I'm going to get until Friday morning" she says, and when the fish does arrive, she treats it in the same way as she does the free range ducks and the lovely east coast lamb.

"I make up five different stock pots, and make jus rather than sauces. Our fish is so fresh, and our produce so good that we don't stray from that policy – leave it alone!".

Thus, salmon may be served with tagliatelle, or be paired with mussels in filo, or those mussels may team with leeks to match some brill, and there may be roasted monkfish, and then some honey and cinnamon ice cream or cassata.

In the Farmgate Café, meantime the buzz will be no less exuberant than out in Midleton. Kay has a policy of only cooking what is for sale downstairs in the market, but she also loves to play around with ingredients others might neglect, concocting dishes such as a Ring farmhouse cheese and mushroom tart.

Kay and Glenna, her head chef, understand the need to make tastes attractive and sinuous, whether making a bowl of Irish stew, a lovely dish of tripe and drisheen or just a bumper salad.

■ OPEN:
Café open 8.30am-5.30pm Mon-Sat
Farm Gate open 9.30am-5.30pm Mon-Sat
7.30pm-late Fri & Sat
(and Thur in high season)

■ AVERAGE PRICE:
Café: Lunch £3-£10; House Wine £10
Farm Gate: Lunch £5, Dinner £20

■ CREDIT CARDS:
Visa, Access/Master

■ NOTES:
Wine Licence. Wheelchair Access
Children – welcome
The Café is in the English Market in Cork, the Farm Gate is in the centre of Midleton.

ISAAC'S BRASSERIE

Canice Sharkey & Michael & Catherine Ryan
48 MacCurtain Street
Cork
Co Cork
Tel: (021) 503805 Fax: 551348

Head Chef: Canice Sharkey

Few restaurants get things right from the day they open their doors, but Isaac's is one of those rare places which not only managed to hit the ground running, but which continues to burn brightly. Michael Ryan and Canice Sharkey hit perfectly the note of accessibility and affordability which has been the keynote of modern Irish eating, and they have reaped the rewards, deservedly.

At lunchtime, with the big tall, brasserie-like room light and bright, it is a splendid space, one of the most charming rooms not just in the city, but in the entire country.

You step inside and it feels just right, and Canice Sharkey's food will be full of suggestions to inspire the appetite: their excellent Caesar salad; some shellfish soup with a soft pink rouille served alongside; some colourful fresh tagliatelle ribboned on the plate and swathed with a red pepper sauce with smoked bacon and cream cheese; the lovely, easy salmon and potato cakes with mayonnaise, that good lamb casserole with flageolet beans and a parmesan crust.

The simplicity and informality of the food suits a simple, speedy bite, but its correctness and stylishness will suit a luridly long excursion with plenty of white wine, a conference with friends that tails off somewhere late in the afternoon.

At dinnertime, with the lights lit and the populous buzz of the diners good and loud, the catholicity of Mr Sharkey's cooking will again seem apt, and able to offer just what you feel like eating, whether that be pheasant with potato and a light butter sauce, a beefy sirloin with rustic spuds and a bearnaise, maybe something simple like a char-grilled burger with a cream and mushroom sauce and cracking fries. Desserts are classic: chocolate St. Emilion; bread and butter pudding; lemon meringue tart, caramel ice cream.

Such an international array of dishes on one menu may suggest that the food will incline to the ersatz, but Mr Sharkey is a controlled cook, and the flavours in his food are as buzzy and happy, and as confident, as the atmosphere in the lovely dining room. The wine list is a masterpiece of concision and selection, and value for money is superb.

■ OPEN:
10am-10.30pm Mon-Sat
6.30pm-9.30pm Sun
■ AVERAGE PRICE:
Lunch £6
Dinner from £14.50
House Wine from £8.95
■ CREDIT CARDS:
Visa, Access/Master, Amex, Diners

■ NOTES:
Wine Licence
Full Wheelchair Access
Children – welcome, high chair
Opposite the Metropole Hotel.

ISLAND COTTAGE (→)

John Desmond & Ellmary Fenton
Heir Island, Skibbereen, Co Cork
Tel: (028) 38102 Fax: 38102

Head Chef: John Desmond

Island Cottage Restaurant turns the conventional wisdom of the restaurant business on its head.

Conventional restaurant wisdom has it that the three most important factors involved in a restaurant are, respectively, location, location, and location.

Island Cottage does have an impressive location. Beautiful, indeed. But, to get there, you must first drive down a long and bendy road, a few miles out of Skibbereen, then take a boat ride, over to Heir Island, and then walk about half a mile up to the little cottage, smack in the middle of this little cusp of land.

And, of course, Heir Island is a terrific success, full to its modest capacity – it is only a single room – during the season. Its success is founded on a number of simple truths that reveal the method behind this seeming madness.

Vitally, the cooking is superb. Indeed, in recent years John Desmond's no-choice menus have shown a chef at the very peak of his powers. A sublime carpaccio of salmon with a fennel mayonnaise might begin dinner, after you have had a drink outside on the patio and watched the sun set in the sky.

Then some duck breast with leek and roast potatoes, the kind of cookery which Mr Desmond does to perfection. If it is true that only the French and the Chinese know how to cook duck, then a dish such as this, and its utter command of technique, reveals John Desmond's long apprenticeship in Burgundy.

And things continue on this stratospheric scale, with a dazzling garden salad, then excellent Gubbeen and Coolea cheeses, and finally a lemon crêpe soufflé which just bowls you over with bliss.

The vivacity of the cooking, importantly, takes its cue from local foods: local cheeses, local fish which Mr Desmond often catches himself, garden herbs. Done like this, the cooking is an aleph of this couple and their method, and from each plate we can see their understanding of the local food culture.

Ellmary Fenton works the front of house with the same sense of discipline and command as John Desmond shows in the cooking. Together, they have created a uniquely wonderful place. There is nowhere else like Heir Island, nowhere else so unequivocal, and so successful on its own terms.

■ OPEN:
Evenings, reservations only
Jun-Sep, Wed-Sun

■ AVERAGE PRICE:
Dinner £17. House Wine from £8

■ CREDIT CARDS:
No Credit Cards

■ NOTES:
Wine Licence
No Wheelchair Access
Take the boat at Cunnamore Pier (signposted from Skibbereen/Ballydehob road). Boat will be arranged when booking. Note there is a charge for boat journey.

THE IVORY TOWER ✪

Seamus O'Connell
The Exchange Buildings
35 Princes Street, Cork, Co Cork
Tel: (021) 274665

Head Chef: Seamus O'Connell

Seamus O'Connell's restaurant is not like other restaurants.

He doesn't cook like other folk, and he doesn't write menus like other folk. His menus are the most extensive, and the most imaginative, you can find, and he changes them twice a day. He doesn't have much time for the niceties of service – you are likely to be handed a glass of wine in here, rather than have it served to you on a tray, for example – and he plays the kind of music which others would consider suicidal for a restaurant: on our last visit it was Miles Davis' tumultuous, brilliant, "Bitches Brew" which was erupting from the speakers, a wholly appropriate choice, all things considered.

Instead, what Mr O'Connell does, each and every day, is to conduct a wild experiment with food and with cooking. He shops, then he and his team cook, and you enter this restaurant with your hunger buds humming with anticipation.

If you love excitement and creativity in food, then you will forgive The Ivory Tower every one of its shortcomings in other areas, and you may very well conclude that Mr O'Connell is the most original talent at work in the country.

The only way to demonstrate his range is to quote from a typical lunchtime menu. There is a Thai prawn bisque with lime leaves. Nordic dilled herring with Atlantic char gravadlax. A salad of warm duck confit with shiitake mushrooms. Prawn and pheasant gyoza. Jalapeno and Desmond tostada. A fricassée of squid Niçoise. A bouillabaisse of gurnard. Cajun blackened shark. Moroccan aubergine charlotte. Pfefferneuse gateau. Passion and fig delice. And there is more.

Impossible to execute? Not for Seamus O'Connell. The charlotte will be perfect, the dilled herring amazing, the tostado amazing, the crab and avocado sushi roll with kim chee which we haven't even mentioned will show his extraordinary grasp of every cuisine.

He is a culinary polymath, who simply works in a parallel universe to every other cook in the country: the other guys are doing landscapes with trees and horses, whilst Seamus is tearing the canvas apart with cubism. Wild, brilliant, unique, and of course not to everyone's taste. But if you hunger for excitement, then just walk up the stairs to the Ivory Tower, abandon any preconceptions, and prepare for the ride.

■ OPEN:
Noon-3pm, 6pm-1pm Tue-Sat
■ AVERAGE PRICE:
Lunch £10. Dinner £17.50-£25
House Wine from £11-£40
■ CREDIT CARDS:
Visa, Access/Master

■ NOTES:
Wine Licence
No Wheelchair Access (but happy to help)
Children – welcome, high chair
Above the Farmhouse cakeshop.

JACQUES

Jacqueline & Eithne Barry
Phoenix Street
Cork
Co Cork
Tel: (021) 277387
Fax: 270634

Chefs:
Jacqueline & Eithne Barry
& Eileen Carey

They just can't stop, Eithne and Jacqueline. After their long tenure in the trade, you would reckon they could sit back, rest on their laurels, take it a bit easy, tread the trusted formula which has seen them through the business so successfully for so long. Not a bit of it.

This restlessness is seen in every aspect of Jacques and, after more than a decade at the stove, the girls are as enthusiastic and as determined to do their best as they have ever been.

Every year sees the sisters initiate changes and developments, the most significant of which was the recent transformation of the room from a rather time-warped ensemble of space into a funky, curvy, colourful room which trades on classic design and colours and which was extremely well achieved. Indeed, this was one of the smartest make-overs in Irish restaurants in recent times, and it worked also to give the whole enterprise a new lease of life.

The cooking, likewise, marches ever on, gradually embracing more lightness and searching out more natural flavours in recent years, whilst offering many of the fashionable concoctions of the day. But if the menu does innovate, it also clings to some of their great staple dishes.

So, you may decide on ribollita with extra virgin olive oil and then Mediterranean chicken with polenta, parmesan, roast vegetables and a basil pesto. But you could also choose a mushroom risotto with Clonakilty black pudding and then traditional roast duck with a potato and apricot stuffing, or a good sirloin with a Café de Paris butter, or an eternal dish such as rack of spring lamb with herbed breadcrumbs, Dijon mustard and a mint jus.

At lunchtime there are lovely fresh things such as a hot pitta bread sandwich with spicy chicken, tomato pickle and a green salad, or crab cakes with a salsa verde.

After nearly fifteen years, they would be entitled to take a rest, but Cork is a better place because they won't, because they can't.

■ OPEN:
Noon-3pm Mon-Fri
6pm-10.30pm Mon-Sat

■ AVERAGE PRICE:
Lunch from £4.90
Dinner from £19.90
House Wine from £10.90

■ CREDIT CARDS:
Visa, Access/Master, Amex, Diners

■ NOTES:
Early Dinner, 2 course, £10.90
Wine Licence
Wheelchair Access, but not to toilets
Children – welcome up to 7.30pm
Turn left at the exit of Imperial Hotel (main entrance), then left again onto Pembroke St, right off Pembroke St to Phoenix St.

LETTERCOLLUM HOUSE ➜

Con McLoughlin & Karen Austin
Timoleague, Co Cork
Tel: (023) 46251 Fax: 46270
e-mail: conmc@iol.ie

Head Chef: Con McLoughlin

The informality of Lettercollum House can come as a surprise to some people. Perhaps they expect something grander from this big, sort-of-sinister house, something more in keeping with other country houses which moulder along on discretion, decorum, and a fondness for times past.

But the lure of Lettercollum for others is not just the splendid cooking of Con and Karen, but also its gleeful sense of originality and its reordering of priorities. Sure, it is a big country house, formerly in religious hands and with the impressive stained glass windows to prove it, but it is run today as a hostel and a restaurant, and the food here is as immediate, as funky, as you will find anywhere in Ireland.

Lettercollum also has an additional bonus, which is never stated but which is a vital aspect of its ambience: it is an idealistic place, designed to offer excellent cooking at terrific prices to all and sundry, in a happy atmosphere. It is democratic.

But idealistic intentions and democratic thinking won't succeed unless the food on the plate is the business, and you don't have to worry about that here. Mr McLoughlin is a fine cook, his style revelling in the fine ingredients he extracts from their walled garden, and he has patiently built up a very distinct culinary profile in recent years.

There is a lovely ruddiness to the food, something about the dishes which satisfies a deep, deep hunger in you. Squid braised in red wine with homemade tagliatelle. A clever pissaladiere tartlet with tzatziki. Their excellent homemade pork terrines. Monkfish with lime and fresh ginger. Tortellini of four cheeses with a tomato butter sauce. Lettercollum pork with white wine and sage. Splendid cooking, special cooking, and if the blackberry delice is on during the blackberry season, then don't miss it.

Everything gets joyfully turned on its head in Lettercollum, everything, that is, except respect for good ingredients, for culinary technique, and a groovy determination that eaters should have a hell of a time and not require a second mortgage to fund that memorable Sunday lunch, that wonderful Friday night with your best friends, that quiet Tuesday dinner. Splendid.

■ OPEN:
7.30pm-9.30pm Wed-Sat, 1pm-3.30pm Sun (seven days high season)

■ AVERAGE PRICE:
Lunch from £12
Dinner from £18.50
House Wine from £10

■ CREDIT CARDS:
Visa, Access/Master, Amex, Diners

■ NOTES:
Wine Licence
Full Wheelchair Access
Children – welcome, high chair
Lettercollum House is off the first road on the right coming out of Timoleague, heading towards Clonakilty.

LISS ARD LAKE LODGE & RESTAURANT

Claudia Meister
Skibbereen, Co Cork
Tel: (028) 22365 Fax: 22839

Head Chef: Stephen Walsh

The cooking in Liss Ard Lake Lodge is unique.

You might explain the singular style of Claudia Meister and her chef Stephen Walsh as deriving from the fact that they use almost no dairy products in their cooking, a move which forces them to re-evaluate almost every standard dish they prepare.

But there is rather more to it than simply playing with a different deck of culinary cards. Ms Meister's cooking is that most unusual thing, a style which is intellectually whole and complete unto itself. This is not the way most chefs work. Most chefs create spins on classic dishes and classic combinations, and then try their hands at a little bit of fusion of different cuisines.

Claudia Meister comes out of somewhere else altogether, her food having enjoyed the intellectual overhaul of a woman who came late to cooking, and who has spent little or no time in professional kitchens. Her cooking is, therefore, a sport of nature.

And the nature bit is important, for her work tries to seize the very essence of an ingredient, the very spirit of the flavour, and then present it in as unalloyed and sympathetic a way as possible. Aided by the fact that they produce much of their own food, Claudia Meister is able to achieve her ambition with stunning effect.

Here is a restaurant where even confirmed carnivores might choose the vegetarian feast – Turk head endive with a plum and ginger dip; terrific miso with hijiki; megatastic noodles with roasted mushrooms; ethereal rosemary sorbet; brilliant roulade of vegetables with pesto and couscous; fab Prosecco sabayon.

But then you might miss the roasted langoustine and crab-filled cherry tomatoes, the roasted kid in its own juice with garden vegetables, the lamb seasoned with Sichuan pepper served with autumn vegetables, or the turbot with a sorrel cream, and the amazing pavé of dark chocolate and mint sabayon, or the great strawberry soufflé.

Service is astute, prices are fair, the wine list is rather interesting, and the dining room rather lovely.

Liss Ard offers breathtaking cooking, cooking which, in its search for sheer perfection, can almost literally take your breath away.

■ OPEN:
7pm-10pm Wed-Mon
■ AVERAGE PRICE:
Dinner from £29. House Wine from £11
■ CREDIT CARDS:
Visa, Access/Master, Amex

■ NOTES:
Wine Licence
Wheelchair Access, but not to toilets
Children – welcome, high chair
Drive through the town of Skibbereen, turning left at the crossroads (signposted Castletownshend). Just outside the town. Follow the road for about 1 mile and you will see the signs to the hotel.

LONGUEVILLE HOUSE ✪

The O'Callaghan family
The President's Restaurant
Mallow
Co Cork
Tel: (022) 47156 Fax: 47459
e-mail: lville@indigo.ie

Head Chef: William O'Callaghan

Two things arise inevitably at the end of dinner in Longueville House.

You say: "God, that was wonderful!".

And you say: "God, how does he do it?"

God might know, but no one else does. Just how does William O'Callaghan create these dishes? Some French friends, who stayed in this spiffing big fairy-cake of a house, were forced to ask themselves the same thing:

"You just wonder what are the tricks that make an apparently didactic dish as 'Roast leg of Longueville lamb and baby vegetables' just sumptuous, and a more risky, glamour-oriented, appetiser like 'Saffron potatoes filled with crab and gratinated with a curry sabayon' so powerfully direct", they wrote.

This is young Mr O'Callaghan's genius. He is one of the foremost kitchen alchemists in the country, able to transform and render anew conventional dishes, able to devise radical interpretations of standards. He can cook like a country man – the Longueville pork has to be tasted to be believed, the Longueville lamb with tarragon sauce is one of the most mesmerising things you can eat in the entire country - and yet he has an ethereality in his work which allows him, for example, to make something basic - such as an avocado mousse - like no other, and which means that desserts here are exemplary: garden apple tart with Calvados ice cream; cracking gratinated hot lemon mousse; lovely poached pear with chocolate vacherin.

"A springy, state-of-the-art cuisine matching a truly heartfelt simplicity", wrote our French friends, and the resolution of this tension, between his love for adventure and his love for ruddiness, is what William O'Callaghan's work achieves. The vivid and precise flavourings of a crab and coconut cake with stir-fried vegetables in ginger, garlic and coriander are contemporary, whilst the parsnip cake paired with loin of venison is ageless.

He can do both perfectly, and his food finds the right forum in the elegance and calm nobility of Longueville, a house which stands on no ceremony, where the local staff are calm and gracious. The local foods, the local folk, and the local lad in the kitchen. Wonderful.

But, how does he do it?

■ **OPEN:**
For non residents dinner if pre booked
28 Feb-21 Dec

■ **AVERAGE PRICE:**
Dinner from £29. House Wine £14

■ **CREDIT CARDS:**
Visa, Access/Master, Amex, Diners

■ **NOTES:**
Full Pub Licence
No Wheelchair Access
Children – welcome, high chair
4 miles west of Mallow on the N72.

OYSTERCATCHER ✪

Bill & Sylvia Patterson
Oysterhaven, nr Kinsale, Co Cork
Tel: (021) 770822 Fax: 770822

Head Chef: Bill Patterson

He may no longer be the spring chicken he once was, and he may even decide some day soon to hang up his ladles and put up his feet, but there is no cook who cooks with more spark and fizz in the kitchen than Bill Patterson, and when the day comes that he finally decides to take it easy, he will be much-missed by food lovers.

Over the last number of years, ever since Bill and Sylvia took over this rather lovely little cottage and transformed it into one of the great gastronomic destinations in the country, Mr Patterson's cooking has won him many friends.

Indeed, this is one of the great characteristics of the Oystercatcher. Tiny, intimate and personal, it is a place where you quickly come to know your hosts, and quickly come to love a style of service – charming, gracious, relaxed – and a style of cooking – persuasive, delicious, enjoyable – which you feel you have been looking for for years.

It is worth stating this fact: this is friendly food, food to fall in love with, and a restaurant to fall in love with. Of course Mr Patterson's work has tremendous polish and chutzpah – the solid sender starters which are the pastry wrapped king prawns with a peanut dip; the dazzling rock oysters with angel hair pasta; succulent woodcock on a crouton; marvellous confit of wild rabbit with a red wine sauce; punchy fresh tuna with pickled lemons and sorrel – but it is first and foremost food to enjoy, food gifted with marvellous flavours thanks to marvellous cooking.

Other chefs with such talent, after such a long career, would be chock-a-block with ego, but Bill Patterson is a professional right to the tip of his sabatier.

What is his secret? Perhaps, even more than the fact that he loves a good time, it is the fact that he loves food. He loves the bounteousness of food and cooking, the generosity, the sharing and, with Sylvia at front of house, we can enjoy the caring as well. Put these things together, and you get a special restaurant, a unique restaurant.

But, it is hard to think of the Irish restaurant scene without Bill Patterson, so we have a feeling there may well be as many retirements and come-backs as Frank Sinatra in the offing.

■ OPEN:
7.15pm-9.15pm Tue-Sat, booking advisable.
Open for reservation only Mar & Oct-Dec.
Open Sun & Mon high season.

■ AVERAGE PRICE:
Dinner from £25.95
House Wine from £10.95

■ CREDIT CARDS:
Visa, Access/Master, Amex

■ NOTES:
Open for lunch for parties of ten or more if pre booked
Wine Licence
Wheelchair Access, but not to toilets
Children – well behaved children welcome
From Kinsale, turn right at the second bridge on Kinsale Cork road. Follow signs to Oysterhaven.

SHIRO JAPANESE DINNER HOUSE

Kei & Werner Pilz
Ahakista, Co Cork
Tel: (027) 87030

Head Chef: Kei Pilz

"This could be Carmel, in California", said a friend with whom we paid a visit to the Shiro.

Indeed it could, but our friend could have picked almost any famous beauty spot in the world to compare to Ahakista and The Shiro.

The elevated site of the house, an old Bishop's palace, overlooks Dunmanus Bay, and enjoys spectacular views. The camellias were in resplendent bloom in the terraced garden, even though it was early in the year and there was little in blossom in the surrounding landscape, proof of how protected this charming village is from the elements. The setting of The Shiro is magical, simply enchanting.

The restaurant has doubled in size in recent times, which is to say it now has four tables instead of the two tables which were all it consisted of for so many years, with three of the tables in an elegant new room at the front of the house.

This was a good idea, as these tables enjoy the view, and it was courageous of Kei and Werner Pilz, who do all of the cooking and serving and running of the restaurant by themselves, to consider such a move at this stage of their lives.

The cooking, by Kei, is as authentic as Japanese food can be when meshed with Irish ingredients, and the menu revolves around constant themes, with an appetiser of various Japanese foods to begin – marinated tofu, sashimi, pickled seaweed – followed by suimono, a clear soup, and then one chooses from an assortment of dishes: sashimi, sushi, masu-yaki, perhaps a mix of styles such as tempura-sashimi.

Mrs Pilz cooks well, and the Shiro continues to exert a powerful spell. But the increase in the number of diners has resulted in some loss of precision in the finishing, and one of the unique features of the restaurant, the stunningly elaborate presentation of the dishes which was an art work in itself – Mrs Pilz is a painter – has now been reduced. The work is still meticulous, and no one else in the country can do it, but those who remember the restaurant from its glory days can't help but be a little deflated. The Shiro has become more like a standard restaurant, rather than the extraordinary and unique dinner house of old. However, there is still nowhere else like it, and you should try it at least once.

■ **OPEN:**
6m-11pm Mon-Sun

■ **AVERAGE PRICE:**
Dinner from £42-£45
House Wine from £16

■ **CREDIT CARDS:**
Visa, Access/Master, Amex, Diners

■ **NOTES:**
Wine Licence
Wheelchair Access
No Children
From Bantry take signs to Durrus, and drive on down the Sheep's Head Peninsular where you will see the gates on your right. The restaurant is well signposted.

THE VINTAGE

Raoul & Seiko de Gendre
Kinsale
Co Cork
Tel: (021) 772502
Fax: 774828

Head Chef: Raoul de Gendre

It is a mark of the exacting, precise business people that they are that, even before the year is out, Raoul and Seiko de Gendre will have produced a programme for the follow-ing year, covering all the special dinners, the wine tastings with visiting winemakers, the festivals and other events which they intend to mark with special menus in The Vintage, for almost the complete 12 months of the year.

Most restaurateurs in Ireland can't think much more than 12 hours ahead of where they are, never mind 12 months.

This sort of planning and professionalism has elevated The Vintage to the status of most consistent performer in Kinsale, the town which describes itself as the "Gourmet Capital of Ireland".

It certainly has many more restaurants than anywhere of a comparable size, but Kinsale has been marked by an unwillingness to trailblaze with its cooking in recent years. A comfortable complacency has set in, the same sort of problem which bedevils places like Killarney and Dingle, with restaurants basically offering the same sort of thing wherever you go, so the dynamism of the de Gendre's is most especially welcome.

The restaurant has always been one of the prettiest in the town, with a romantic, cosy atmosphere in its cloistering, low-ceilinged space, and the cooking with its mixture of accomplishment and familiarity offers the right food in the right place.

They can do very classic things such as fillets of black sole sautéed belle meuniere with a lemon butter sauce, a dish which scores perfectly in capturing unalloyed, simple and expressive flavours, whilst one of the newer standards such as scallops with vanilla will again be precise, effective. Their oven roasted barbary duck will be served with a confit of its leg, offering two totally different and complementary tastes from the bird, whilst smoked pork is cooked with apples and calvados and served with Clonakilty black pudding.

Best of all, there is no unnecessary fiddling about with the food: it speaks for itself.

Prices for dinner have become ever-keener since the de Gendre's took over, and they have an interesting policy of using many visiting chefs during the year.

■ OPEN:
6.45pm-10pm Mon-Sun Apr-Oct
Off season closed Sun

■ AVERAGE PRICE:
Dinner £26-£37
House Wine £16.50

■ CREDIT CARDS:
Visa, Access/Master, Amex, Diners

■ NOTES:
Restaurant Licence
No Wheelchair Access
Children – welcome
In the centre of Kinsale.

CASTLE MURRAY HOUSE

Thierry & Claire Delcros
Dunkineely, Co Donegal
Tel: (073) 37022 Fax: 37330

Head Chef: Thierry Delcros

Thierry Delcros's restaurant has been one of the most inspiring success stories in recent years.

Having quietly worked his way around this place and that, gifting other people's restaurants and hotels with the benefit of his exquisitely attuned skills, M. Delcros and his wife Claire opened Castle Murray at the end of 1989.

The news of their good food spread like wildfire, not just in Donegal – a county where, on all too many occasions, you would wish that it would be possible that you could eat the view, for the view would be delicious, and dinner would not – but also across the border into the North.

The reasons for this success are instantly recognisable: he devoted himself to a local audience and their needs and demands – Sunday lunch in here lasts all day! – a lack of pretentiousness, superb food at good prices and the ability, because those prices are so keen, to stay overnight in one of their rooms and thus make a decent night of it. This is the simple concept of the Restaurant with Rooms, seen here at its best.

M. Delcros' cooking remains devotedly French but, like the cooking of Dunworley Cottage, in County Cork, for example, where the influence is Swedish, his work proves the perfect marriage between Irish ingredients – wild game birds (M. Delcros is a hunter), fresh fish and shellfish, bio-dynamically grown vegetables, fresh eggs from run-around chickens – and the precise strictures of classic techniques.

He doesn't innovate very much, hardly at all – there will be pâtés, effete soups, fish with sauces, meats with sauces, and you can have a dinner as simple as onion soup, then a grilled sirloin steak and some ices to finish if you wish, but it is in the extraction of flavour and the respect for balance in a dish which is his signature.

He is also disciplined, producing cooking which is consistent, producing cooking which tastes right, from Tournedos façon Rossini, to Braised Brill with Leeks, from McSweyne's Bay Blue Lobster, to Fresh Pasta au Poisson.

Prices are very keen, and the wine list is absorbing and unusual. On a busy night service can get a little strung-out, but there is always the startlingly beautiful view to regard, and this is food worth waiting for.

■ **OPEN:**
7pm-9.30pm Mon-Sat, 3pm-8pm Sun
■ **AVERAGE PRICE:**
Lunch £13
Dinner £18-£26
House Wine £8
■ **CREDIT CARDS:**
Visa, Access/Master

■ **NOTES:**
Restaurant Licence
Wheelchair Access
Children – welcome, high chair
Signposted after the village of Dunkineely, heading west out of Donegal towards Killybegs.

KEALY'S SEAFOOD BAR

James & Tricia Kealy
Greencastle, Co Donegal
Tel: (077) 81010 Fax: 81010

Head Chef: James Kealy

There is a muteness about the menu in Kealy's Seafood Bar, a little place close to the pier in Greencastle, Co Donegal, which is somehow splendidly reassuring.

Seafood cocktail. Greencastle chowder. Poached fillet of cod with Stilton. Poached fillet of hake with a saffron butter sauce. Whole sole on the bone, meunière.

And there isn't too much about the bar and the dining room to give the game away, either, though there is a very nifty bar, salvaged from a dancehall in Derry, apparently. There are some smart canvases by local artists on the walls, but, all told, there is little to get too excited about.

And this is Kealy's secret, of course. In James and Tricia Kealy's seafood bar they do good stuff, and they do it well, and they don't make a song and dance about it. There is a confidence at the core of this little place which you see in the most obvious of dishes. They make a lentil soup which is pure dynamite, the fleshy bite of the lentils beefed up with carrots, whilst the Greencastle chowder is another dish which shows excellent balance, not too creamy, not overdosed with tomatoes, the flesh of the fish still firm and satisfying.

Main courses understand the laws of fish cookery, which is to say that if you have a good piece of fresh fish, then:

1. Don't overcook it, and:
2. Don't muck about with it.

Grilled fillet of wild salmon comes with a lime butter which is a true friend to the fish, whilst some cod in crispy batter will be just perfect, accompanied by grandiose portions of chips.

Some good cinnamon ice cream, some good coffee, a modest bill, and you leave with the feeling that it would be rather nice to have a little weekend place here on the edge of the Foyle, as so many of the bourgeoisie of the North do.

And then you could nip into Kealy's most weekends, and work your way through that modest menu, trying the lemon sole with a mustard beurre blanc, and the smoked haddock florentine, and the john dory with anchovy butter.

And this lovely cooking is enjoyed in the company of happy folk who know just how lucky they are to have this little gem of a place, just down the road, on the waterfront.

■ **OPEN:**
12.30pm-3pm 7pm-9.30pm Mon-Sun
(closed Mon-Wed off season)

■ **AVERAGE PRICE:**
Lunch £10.
Dinner £17.50
House Wine £9.50

■ **CREDIT CARDS:**
Visa, Access/Master, Amex, Diners

■ **NOTES:**
Bar Licence
Wheelchair Access
Children – welcome lunch and early evening, high chair
On the seafront, opposite the harbour.

AYUMI-YA

Japanese Restaurant,
Newpark Centre, Newtownpark Ave Blackrock, Co Dublin
Tel: (01) 283 1767
Head Chef: Lian Wu Wang

Japanese Steakhouse, 132 Lower Baggot Street, Dublin 2
Tel: (01) 662 0233 Fax: 662 0221

Head Chef: Jennifer Glynn

Like all of the very best restaurants, the focus of Yoichi Hoashi's two Ayumi-Yas is centred firmly on the needs and desires of the customer.

As the restaurants have progressed and developed over the years – and the Blackrock restaurant is now an elder statesman of the Dublin scene – Mr Hoashi has worked to make this dazzling, brilliant cuisine more accessible to the people of Dublin. Unlike other ethnic restaurants, the Ayumi-Yas are very good at both explaining the cooking, and how to approach it, and the staff are superbly helpful. Indeed, they have a ministering kindness which serves to make everyone feel relaxed and comfortable.

The Steakhouse offers the cuisine of Japan in a relaxed, noodle-house atmosphere, which the basement setting suits perfectly, but there is also a sushi menu to complement the noodles, and the teppan steaks, and the kushi-age, and there is – vitally – a brilliant bento box service, whereby the food of the Ayumi-Ya can be taken away in a see-through box, the compartments filled with finger lickin' titbits. This is the best takeaway food in the city.

The Blackrock restaurant, then, is more formal, with traditional seating areas, and there are more extensive menus, including sushi and osashimi menus.

There are certain things which you should definitely not miss: the buckwheat noodles with tempura is one; the wonderful San Francisco sashimi; the dazzlingly fresh yellow fin tuna; the amazing cured salmon with ginger and the great char-grilled salmon; the soba noodles with chicken.

There are teppan-yaki tables here for those who like to sit right at the cooker, and the service is sublime: cosseting, caring, altogether charming. These are indispensable, authentic restaurants.

■ OPEN:
Restaurant: 6pm-11.30pm Mon-Sat, 5.30pm-9.45pm Sun
Steakhouse: 12.30pm-2.30pm, 6pm-11.30pm Mon-Sat

■ AVERAGE PRICE:
Restaurant: Dinner from £16.50
House Wine £10.25
Steakhouse: Lunch £6.30-£10.95
Dinner £10.95-£13.95 + service

■ CREDIT CARDS:
Visa, Access/Master, Amex, Diners

■ NOTES:
Early Bird dinner, £11.30, in Restaurant
Steakhouse: Wine Licence
Restaurant: Restaurant Licence
Wheelchair Access in Restaurant only
Children – welcome until 8pm, high chair, special menu, £6
For the Restaurant, access to Newtownpark Ave from either N11 (Stillorgan dual carriageway) or Stradbrook Rd. Restaurant located in small centre beside the Playwright Inn.
For the Steakhouse, it is on the corner of

CHAMELEON

Carol Walshe & Vincent Vis
1 Fownes Street Lower, Dublin 2
Tel: (01) 671 0362

Head Chef: Vincent Vis

There has always been a goodness about Vincent Vis's cooking, a sense of freshness and purity which made it extra enjoyable. Ever since he decided to explore his own back pages, and concoct Indonesian dishes, and ever since he and Carol Walshe pooled their respective talents to open up the simple space that is The Chameleon, they have gone from strength to strength, thanks to charming food, which quickly found its feet, and charming service, in a restaurant which is a quintessential Temple Bar space.

Mr Vis and Ms Walshe began on a shoestring in a single room, and as things have improved they have gradually cultivated the entire building on Fownes Street, room by room, floor by floor. It is worth stating this, because recently a whole lot of folk with too much money and no taste have opened places in Temple Bar. Chameleon isn't like those places: it has progressed organically, it represents the best efforts of two talented people, it succeeds because it is unique. They may not have much money, but they do have good taste.

Vincent Vis cooks Indonesian food with a true understanding of the complexities and comforts which the dishes must articulate. Rijst-tafel, the "rice-table" which offers a sample of eight different dishes, accompanied by eight different condiments, offers the familiar – a saté of chicken, the meat skewered and cloaked with a peanut sauce which is delightfully intense and pointed in flavour – and the esoteric.

There will be Bami Goreng, where Chinese noodles are fried with pork, ginger, garlic and beansprouts, the tastes surprisingly Asiatic and beautifully achieved, whilst the coconut flavours vary considerably. With Beef Rendang the coconut milk is deliciously seductive, whilst with Sambal Goreng Telor, the coconut melds with a rich sauce of macadamia nuts in a simple dish of eggs and tomatoes. Sambal Goreng Kool, by contrast, has Indonesian spices and coconut milk as the dressing for fried white cabbage, a dish which is quintessential Vincent Vis: exotic, earthy, somehow bursting with health.

The Chameleon is a smashing place, somewhere which fizzes with bonhomie and that raucous Dublinesque lust for life. In an area which has all too many places which are ersatz, here is a taste of the real thing.

■ OPEN:
5.30pm-11pm Wed-Sun (till 10pm Sun)
■ AVERAGE PRICE:
Dinner from £10.50-£20.50
House Wine from £10.75
■ CREDIT CARDS:
Visa, Access/Master

■ NOTES:
Wine Licence
Wheelchair Access, but not to toilets
Children – welcome
Almost overlooking the River Liffey, in Dublin's Temple Bar.

THE CHINA-SICHUAN

David Hui
4 Lower Kilmacud Rd, Stillorgan
Co Dublin
Tel: (01) 288 4817 Fax: 288 0882

Head Chef: Mr Lee

The sweet and sour is the barometer.

This glorious dipping sauce, one of the trademarks of Chinese cooking, is either one of the best things you have ever eaten – not too sweet and sticky, not too sour and shocking – or one of the great culinary travesties of the modern age, a glop festooned with bits of pineapple which gags you with its viscosity.

It says all one needs to know about David Hui's China-Sichuan restaurant, in Stillorgan, that a dish you would be petrified to order elsewhere is one of the first things you order when you sit down in here.

Served with deep fried pieces of chicken, or with monkfish, sea trout, pork fillet or prawns, the sweet and sour sauce is perfectly judged, perfectly poised, just right. For this is Chinese cooking without the clichés invented for bland Western palates.

The roll-call of dishes eaten over the years shows a relentless discipline and effectiveness in the kitchen: the wonderful smoked duckling; the terrific coffee-odoured thrill of the hot and sour soup; the great dumplings with a spicy chilli sauce or perhaps a dense black dipping sauce; the exciting tangle of tastes in the monkfish with cashews; the great simplicity of some stir-fried bak choi; the intensity of flavour of the fried shredded pork fillet with garlic sauce; the cooling delight of the almond bean curd.

Aside from the charm of the food, the great benefit of being a regular at the China-Sichuan – and this is a Chinese restaurant with very many regular customers – is the fact that getting to know Tim, the delightful waiter, and his colleagues, can allow you to step outside the menu.

The dish of braised hot and spicy bean curd, for example, is one of their vegetarian specialities. But, if asked, they will also serve this with finely chopped beef and a dressing of coriander, a version which is closer in tone to the classic dish.

Both are terrific, but the willingness of the kitchen to improvise and invent for you is one of the unique things about the China-Sichuan. They may have been in business a long time, but there is nothing jaded about their work.

Allied to the trueness and the variety of tastes in all the dishes, it makes the China-Sichuan the most addictive Chinese restaurant in Dublin.

■ OPEN:
12.30pm-2.30pm Mon-Fri, 1pm-2.30pm Sun, 6pm-11pm Mon-Sun

■ AVERAGE PRICE:
Lunch £8-£10
Dinner from £17.50
House Wine from £9.25

■ CREDIT CARDS:
Visa, Access/Master, Amex, Diners

■ NOTES:
Wine Licence
Wheelchair Access
Children – welcome, high chair
The restaurant is 100 yards from the Stillorgan Shopping Centre, on the Kilmacud Rd, in the midst of some shops.

THE COMMONS

Michael Fitzgerald
Newman House, 85/86
St Stephen's Green, Dublin 2
Tel: (01) 475 2597/478 0530
Fax: 478 0551

Head Chef: Sebastian Masi

The Commons is a singular Dublin restaurant, inasmuch as it represents the vision of a proprietor – Michael Fitzgerald – who is not himself a chef, and as different cooks have come and gone from the kitchens of The Commons, Mr Fitzgerald's desire to run a top-class, expensive and luxurious restaurant has been clung to determinedly.

It is a restaurant where serenity is the keynote. Nothing, but nothing, disturbs the easeful flow of the way in which they do what they do in this stylish basement, with its vista out onto calm gardens.

Nothing disrupts the poise of the room and the poise of the staff. A pacific, almost zen-like, abstractedness embraces the styling, the service, the raison d'être.

You can criticise this, and wish that the restaurant was funkier – a reviewer once wrote that, "One found oneself longing for a nice rowdy table who drank more than they meant to, constantly interrupted each other and laughed too loud at each others' jokes" – and you might wish that the food was punchier in taste and more exotic, not just so totally tasteful, so serene, so restrained.

But to want The Commons to be something other than what Michael Fitzgerald has directed it to be from the day it opened its doors, is to miss the point. It is in not being rowdy that The Commons works.

Its formality is its greatest strength. Its sublimation of any overt personality, any particular sense of place or "Irishness", is something it strives to achieve, and something it does achieve.

It is poised, and precise. It is where you go when entertaining – clients from out of town, that aunt you haven't seen for years and who you hope will bequeath you some money, to celebrate a success in some exam or some promotion. And, because they know that you have business of some nature or other on your mind, the staff never intrude, and they make sure that nothing intrudes.

The cooking is just one more facet of this serenity. It trades off classical dishes with modern innovations and Irish gestures – roast monkfish in bacon with colcannon; steamed salmon with coriander butter; foie gras and grilled black pudding with a pear purée – and its luxuriousness and correctness seduces quietly. Like everything else.

■ OPEN:
12.30pm-2.15pm Mon-Fri
7pm-10.15pm Mon-Sat

■ AVERAGE PRICE:
Lunch £18 + 15%. Dinner from £32 + £15%
House Wine from £16

■ CREDIT CARDS:
Visa, Access/Master, Amex, Diners

■ NOTES:
Restaurant Licence
No Wheelchair Access
Children – no facilities
In the basement of Newman House.

COOKES CAFÉ

John Cooke
14 Sth William Street
Dublin 2
Tel: (01) 679 0536/7/8
Fax: 679 0546

Head Chef: John Cooke

When John Cooke's café burst onto the Dublin scene a few years back, it traded not merely on the fact that it was the most fashionable restaurant in town, but also on a very modern, cool style of cooking, which fused traditional Italian pasta dishes with an array of American-influenced gestures.

It remains a deeply fashionable place, though the gradual extensions of the main dining room and the opening of the upstairs room, has meant that it is definitely less self-conscious than in the past. But what is interesting, regarding the food, is the way in which it has become more formal and classical, has slowly carved out a more distinct personality.

Certain dishes which made their mark early on are staples by now – angel hair vongole; the rich tortelloni au gratin; the intriguing olive oil dip for their fine breads; their knock-out Caesar salad, the grilled asparagus with Parmesan – and these have now been joined by classics such as tomato and mozzarella salad; dover sole meuniere; aged grilled sirloin of beef with balsamic vinegar and fondant potatoes.

And as the restaurant has progressed, John Cooke has increasingly taken a back seat in the kitchen, concentrating on the other aspects of his empire which includes two shops and a bakery.

This has allowed his young chefs, such as Eleanor Walsh, Harry McKeogh, Ann Marie Tobin and others, to bring their styles to bear on the make-up of the menus.

It's a smart move by the proprietor, for the injection of new blood has meant the restaurant has retained its vigour, its energy.

So the conventional grilled breast of chicken might be served one day with a grilled pineapple and papaya salsa, or maybe with grilled Mediterranean vegetables. Veal kidney might appear in a salad with fried celeriac, rather than sautéed in a brandy, mustard and cream sauce. The scallops might come with Noilly Prat and a tomato concasse, or with angel hair pasta and a chervil butter sauce.

This ability to ring the changes is typical of the nature of Cooke's Café, which has always been a progressive organisation, unwilling to tie itself to any particular personality – despite its name. It is a valuable part of the Dublin scene.

■ OPEN:
12.30pm-3.30pm, 6pm-11pm Mon-Sat
■ AVERAGE PRICE:
Lunch £14.95 + 12.5%. Dinner from £25
House Wine from £12.50 + 12.5%
■ CREDIT CARDS:
Visa, Access/Master, Amex, Diners

■ NOTES:
Wine Licence
Wheelchair Access, but not to toilets
Children – welcome if well behaved
Parallel to Grafton Street, directly opposite the entrance to Powerscourt Townhouse Centre.

LE COQ HARDI

John & Catherine Howard
35 Pembroke Road, Dublin 4
Tel: (01) 668 4130/668 8070

Head Chef: John Howard

There was a period, some years back, when the new age of austerity which descended on Dublin seemed to make John and Catherine Howard's Le Coq Hardi somewhat unfashionable.

During the high-rolling years of the 1980s, this was perhaps the quintessential Dublin restaurant, the place that proved the zeitgeist of the city. Grand and glorious, patronised by the great and the good and others with plenty of dosh, Le Coq Hardi was the place to be.

But the leaner years served to make this unapologetic womb of rich cooking and rare wines appear as if it belonged back with Escoffier.

And then, come the late 1990s, Dublin becomes Boom City Europe. And the Coq – freshly re-liveried after a fire caused it to close for a few months – is back in fashion.

John and Catherine Howard have ridden these changes over the years by sticking to their vision of a grand restaurant, come what may. Whilst the economic circumstances of the city have altered, the truth about the Coq is that little there has changed.

There have always been sweet elements of subterfuge to be found here, undermining the image of a bourgeois blow-out temple, for Le Coq Hardi is not as much of a cliché as it appears.

For one thing the food, which trumpets itself as a faithful acolyte of the classical French school, actually has more in common with cuisine paysanne than with cuisine bourgeois.

Very obvious dishes are made with relish here: king scallops with bacon and a potato cake; leek and potato soup with smoked haddock; the famous Coq Hardi smokies; rack of Wicklow lamb served with clapshot; beef stroganoff; beef with colcannon and an Irish whiskey sauce.

This is not really a surprise, for John Howard has never lost touch with the rootsiness which underlies his cooking. There may be an irony in the fact that such relatively simple food carries such high prices, but this is explained by the grandness of the surroundings.

Over the years the style of cooking has, of course, lightened, but this is the only major change this Dublin institution has made to its enduring style.

The wine list in the Coq is an extraordinary thing. Enormous, expensive, and quite enthralling, and ready to be plundered by the plump wallets of Boom City Europe.

■ **OPEN:**
12.30pm-2.30pm Mon-Fri,
7pm-11pm Mon-Sat

■ **AVERAGE PRICE:**
Lunch £18-£21. Dinner from £33
House Wine from £16

■ **CREDIT CARDS:**
Visa, Access/Master, Amex, Diners

■ **NOTES:**
Restaurant Licence
No Wheelchair Access
Children – welcome if well behaved
Junction of Pembroke Rd & Wellington Pk.

L'ECRIVAIN ✪

Derry & Sallyanne Clarke
112 Lower Baggot Street
Dublin 2
Tel: (01) 661 1919 Fax: 661 0617

Head Chef: Derry Clarke

There is nothing more thrilling, more beautiful, more enjoyable and more satisfying than a restaurant where everything – cooking, service, ambience, character – suddenly hits top gear, as people find their niche, refine their work, and discover that they are in the right place at just the right time.

Derry and Sallyanne Clarke's L'Ecrivain is the right restaurant in the right place at the right time.

For many people this has been the great Dublin restaurant of recent years, a powerhouse of good food going from strength to strength to strength. It is a quintessentially Irish place, thanks to the marvellous service of Sallyanne Clarke and Ray Hingston, and thanks to the generous, flavour-drenched, powerful cooking of Derry Clarke.

Mr Clarke was always a good cook, but something extraordinary happened to him when L'Ecrivain moved to bigger, brighter premises a few years back. Coping with bigger numbers meant simplifying his style, and in so doing he uncovered a very distinct and singular way of cooking.

He no longer likes to place food under or on top of other foods, in the modern style, preferring instead to aim for concentrated flavours by isolating a main ingredient and then complementing it with suitable partner flavours.

We might place his work in context by saying that the chef to whom he could most accurately be compared is the great English cook, Simon Hopkinson. Like Hoppy, Mr Clarke loves gutsy, intense flavours, he loves cooking which is very logical, which seeks affinities between ingredients, and which delights in transforming simple things into splendid dishes.

But he also has the skill to make things taste not just distinct, but vivid: magnificent char-grilled entrecote with roasted red peppers and a Café de Paris butter; wallopping roasted venison with a star anise fumé; great roasted Toulouse sausage with braised red cabbage; the celebrated baked rock oysters with cabbage and bacon and a Guinness sabayon; the searing assault of seared scallops with garlic, ginger and a chilli dressing.

Here is cooking to fall in love with, and happily everything else about L'Ecrivain is just as dynamic as Derry Clarke's cooking. Here is a restaurant performing nothing less than magic.

■ OPEN:
12.30pm-2.30pm Mon-Fri,
6.30pm-11pm Mon-Sat

■ AVERAGE PRICE:
Lunch £12.50-£16.50. Dinner from £28
House Wine from £12

■ CREDIT CARDS:
Visa, Access/Master, Amex, Diners

■ NOTES:
Restaurant Licence
Wheelchair Access
Children – welcome if well behaved
Through archway beside Lad Lane.

ELEPHANT & CASTLE ➔

Liz Mee & John Hayes
18 Temple Bar, Dublin 2
Tel: (01) 679 3121 Fax: 679 1399

Head Chef: Liz Mee

It is given to very few people to change the habits of a nation, but Liz Mee and John Hayes changed the eating habits of Dubliners from the very day they opened the doors of the Elephant & Castle.

For the first time in the city, here was a restaurant which acted almost like a neighbourhood restaurant – affordable, accessible, spontaneous, energised, open at the times you want it to be open – even though it was in the centre of town.

The old Dublin restaurant imprimaturs of expense and exclusivity were blown out of the water, along with the idea that you needed to have gone to cheffing school to work in a kitchen. In here, they prefer career jumpers, who have a passion for food, over egotistical laddies with a culinary certificate. This, indeed, has been one of their most important innovations, and combined with the abolition of the autocratic "head chef" idea, it has allowed the E&C to remain flexible, innovative.

But the trump card which Liz and John brought to the E&C was cooking of an exactingly high quality, a quality which, given the huge numbers of people they serve every day of the week, is remarkably consistent.

First thing in the morning – for a poor woman's omelette with croutons and a mug of coffee, perhaps – it is just right. For a late-night dinner – gorgeous stir-fried beef with chillies and shiitake mushrooms; smoked salmon salad with watercress and daikon radish – with a bottle of rich red wine from South West France, it is perfection itself, just the place to romance and gossip and enjoy food which suits your mood perfectly.

The basic menu of the E&C is so successful, and so packed with dishes that you never tire of eating – just how many times have you ordered the spicy chicken wings now? how many burgers have you eaten over the years? – that it has only been tampered with delicately since they opened.

The menu works in tandem with an array of daily specials, described on the blackboard. These can produce stunning dishes, as they usually represent a chance for someone in the kitchen to flex their muscles and show just what they can do.

The E&C is, in many ways, not just the quintessential Temple Bar restaurant, but the quintessential modern Irish restaurant. It has changed everything, for the better.

■ OPEN:
8am-11.30pm Mon-Thur, 8am-midnight Fri, 10.30am-midnight Sat, noon-11.30pm Sun

■ AVERAGE PRICE:
Lunch £4-£10
Dinner from £15-£20
House Wine from £10.25

■ CREDIT CARDS:
Visa, Access/Master, Amex

■ NOTES:
Restaurant Licence
Wheelchair Access
Children – welcome
Behind the Central Bank.

LES FRERES JACQUES

Jean-Jacques & Suzy Caillebet
74 Dame Street
Temple Bar
Dublin 2
Tel: (01) 679 4555 Fax: 679 4725

Head Chef: Jean-Jacques Caillebet

French peasant soup. Saddle of lamb baked in puff pastry. Lobster ravioli with a fillet of turbot. Sole cooked on the bone. Terrine of river pike. Crème brûlée. Vanilla bavarois.

These are the sorts of things they do in Les Freres Jacques. They do them right, and they have been doing them right for years. It's the sort of place which almost makes critics redundant, for here is a restaurant with a seamless, ageless style and good food.

There are a lot of grace notes to be found amongst these dishes, and a lot of enjoyment flows from them. If you ever wondered how and why certain dishes attain classic status, here is the restaurant to show you both why, and how.

This is why there are plenty of judicious people who will select Les Freres Jacques as their favourite Dublin restaurant. They may point to various factors, but the truth is that the restaurant is a place which weaves a little spell.

Walk down the little lane and through the door, and the restaurant invites you in with that dim-lit light that suggests London oyster bars tucked up quiet lanes, or Roman trattorias tucked behind raggedy walls. It all suggests privacy and cosseting and pleasure, an indulgence, something and someplace special.

This may be why it is so popular with solo diners, folk who appreciate and enjoy the efficient and uncondescending way in which the food is served.

For special occasions, and especially for business lunching, the restaurant has that assured rhythm which derives from experience and confidence, but they don't let it slip into swagger, and their Gallic correctness has, over the years, been tempered with an Irish affability. It is a very French restaurant, but it is very definitely in Dublin.

And the food is almost always effective: a mussel and fennel soup; millefeuille of roast lamb and potato; lobster flamed with Irish whiskey. They do not innovate, preferring instead to ensure things are achieved correctly, and are unconcerned about the young blades and trailblazers who have changed the capital's culinary stance.

There is a place in every city for Les Freres Jacques, and they know it. So do you.

■ **OPEN:**
12.30pm-2.30pm Mon-Fri, 7.30pm-10.30pm Mon-Thur, 7.30pm-11pm Fri & Sat

■ **AVERAGE PRICE:**
Lunch from £13
Dinner from £20
House Wine from £10.15

■ **CREDIT CARDS:**
Visa, Access/Master, Amex, Diners

■ **NOTES:**
Wine Licence
No Wheelchair Access
Children – no facilities
A few doors up from the Olympia Theatre on Dame Street, opposite Dublin Castle.

GIROLLES

Gary & Helen Morris
64 South William Street
Dublin 2
Tel: (01) 679 7699 Fax: 493 9880

Head Chef: Gary Morris

Girolles might be described as the little restaurant with the big flavours.

A tiny twin set of rooms which you step down into from the rag trade offices of South William Street, the restaurant underwent various incarnations before Gary and Helen Morris moved here and opened up shop.

Mr Morris had been working with Derry Clarke in L'Ecrivain before the move, and he brought with him his mentor's love of clean, agrestic flavours, and a search for logical pairings and matchings with food.

But if there were some borrowed elements when he first traded on his own, Mr Morris quickly forged his own style in this little space, with everything centred around duets and duos.

There is firstly the duo of a man and his wife, for Mrs Morris is as efficient as her husband, and she is responsible for the duet of food and wine utilising her role as sommelier to strike sparks off his cooking. Finally, there is Mr Morris' search for twins in his culinary work. Everything Gary Morris cooks looks, then, to find an echo of the principal ingredient in another element on the plate, and this makes his food not only clever, but very well conceived and convincing. It also makes it great fun, and produces cooking which you feel you could eat every day of your life.

He will adjust classics like celery soup with the logical addition of blue cheese, and place shards of shellfish amidst the perfectly cooked grains of arborio rice in his risotto – praised by many folk as amongst the best risottos in town. A champagne sabayon is perfect with seared scallops, and his delicious breast of pheasant comes with a tiny game pie and the perfect splash of truffle oil.

But this isn't just smart cooking, half in love with its own intelligence. Mr Morris loves rustic flavours too much to lose sight of the fact that his strength lies with coaxing unadulterated goodness out of his chosen ingredients: smoked salmon with poached egg and bulghur; mussel broth with saffron and barley; Wicklow lamb with white haricot beans, smoked bacon and colcannon.

Wisely, Mr Morris has chosen a quiet path for his work, and he is not a media darling. He is just a fine cook, who runs a fine place.

■ **OPEN:**
12.30pm-2.30pm Mon-Fri, 6pm-11pm Tue-Sun (till 10pm Sun)
■ **AVERAGE PRICE:**
Lunch £12.50
Dinner £21.60
House Wine from £10.95
■ **CREDIT CARDS:**
Visa, Access/Master, Amex, Diners

■ **NOTES:**
Wine Licence
No Wheelchair Access (but happy to help)
Children – welcome, high chair with advance notice.
Sth William St runs parallel with Grafton St.

RESTAURANT PATRICK GUILBAUD

P Guilbaud & G Lebrun
St. James's Place, Baggot Street Lower, Dublin 2
Tel: (01) 676 4192 Fax: 6610052

Head Chef: Guillaume Lebrun

Patrick Guilbaud's eponymous restaurant has trail-blazed for many years now, setting standards with an iron-headed determination, carving out a reputation as a restaurant which is reliable, efficient, ambitious.

It manages all of these things with ease, for here is a restaurant which operates like a machine, producing food of high standards, serving it efficiently and charging very high prices for it.

But, sometimes, when you look around this smart room at dinner-time and see the clientele which RPG attracts – the ageing bourgeoisie, the impressible folk who choose where they eat by virtue of exclusivity and expense – you realise that RPG has been left behind. Increasingly, this seems like a restaurant which has been outpaced by its younger rivals.

Where are the young people? Where are the movers and shakers and food-lovers who search out the good food and the good time Dublin has to offer? Elsewhere, obviously.

If they are elsewhere, then it is for simple reasons. If the menu proposes white asparagus with truffles, served warm, and a dish of green asparagus with a single, flavourless piece of truffle arrives with a hollandaise, one is entitled to an explanation, especially as this little collection of sprigs is costing no less than £14.

But no explanation is forthcoming as to the disappearance of the white asparagus and its replacement with the green shoots.

This sort of towering arrogance explains the difficulty people, and critics, have with RPG. It doesn't exist for its customers, but exists for them to pay homage to it. The staff behave as if their only responsibility to their customers is to ferry out food which, like their behaviour, is above criticism.

There are fine points, of course – a splendid ravioli with lobster and a curried coconut sauce carried off perfectly, or flawlessly roasted duck.

But dinner in RPG can also show many faults, a wild mushroom pudding with some crubeens is dull; a tian of aubergines flavourless, and at these prices one expects more, and one can find more elsewhere.

RPG made sense in the past but, today, when one has come to expect creativity and spontaneity in top-flight restaurant cooking, eating here can feel like eating in a museum.

■ OPEN:
12.30pm-2.30pm
7.30pm-10.15pm Tue-Sat
■ AVERAGE PRICE:
Lunch £22
Dinner from £35
House Wine from £17-£25
■ CREDIT CARDS:
Visa, Access/Master, Amex, Diners

■ NOTES:
Full Pub Licence
Wheelchair Access
Children – welcome, high chair
In a laneway behind the Bank of Ireland on Baggot St.

MERMAID CAFÉ

Ben Gorman & Mark Harrell
69/70 Dame Street, Temple Bar
Dublin 2
Tel: (01) 670 8236 Fax: 6708205

Head Chef: Ben Gorman

The Mermaid quickly became the grooviest restaurant in town, after Ben Gorman and Mark Harrell unveiled its iconoclastic style to the Dublin public.

A long room with an open kitchen at the end, it draws stylistic influences from a vague New England tradition, from which it has excised any trace of Shaker self-denial. So the simplicity of their wooden furniture, white walls and stripped pine floor is curiously luxurious, rather than merely efficient.

If the style is iconoclastic, so is the cooking. What is most enjoyable about the Mermaid is the sense of true endeavour about it, the sense of immediate and unmediated creativity in the food and the working of the place.

The food is good, but one of the reasons why it is good is because it is never slick. None of the chichi decoration and elaboration of bourgeois restaurants can be found in Ben Gorman's work: it is ruddy and real, and greatly enjoyable. Other critics and guidebooks would dismiss this fact but, as the Bridgestone books tend to be rather iconoclastic themselves, we rather like it. It is food with personality, and it is served in a room with personality by young people with personality. If you can't respect that, then you're probably someone who doesn't like Jimi Hendrix either.

"Everything is home-made", they declare at the bottom of the menus, and it is. Something simple like honey roast ham with a herb mash will be just perfect, the smart idea of adding some pomegranate seeds to a garnish of mushrooms successfully achieved. The pan-fried monkfish with a lobster sauce and roasted peppers is great, the braised veal sweetbreads with saffron and jasmin rice spot on. Already there are certain fixed standards on the menu: New England crab cakes with piquant mayonnaise; mussel chowder with celery biscuits; the sweetbreads; the chicken breast with risotto.

Desserts have a lovely, up-front style: prune and Armagnac frozen yogurt; pecan pie with maple ice cream; blueberry steamed pudding with custard.

Of course they make mistakes, but the mistakes are small and the successes are considerable. Great music, great service, great fun.

■ **OPEN:**
Noon-2.30pm, 7pm-11pm Tue-Sat

■ **AVERAGE PRICE:**
Lunch from £12-£15
Dinner from £20
House Wine from £10

■ **CREDIT CARDS:**
Visa, Access/Master, Amex, Diners

■ **NOTES:**
Early Bird dinner, £11.30, in Restaurant
Steakhouse: Wine Licence
Restaurant: Restaurant Licence
Wheelchair Access in Restaurant only
Children – welcome until 8pm, high chair, special menu, £6

MORELS BISTRO

Alan O'Reilly
Morel's Bistro, 18 Glasthule Road
Sandycove, Co Dublin
Tel: (01) 230 0210 Fax: 230 0466

Morel's Bistro, 14-18 Lower
Leeson Street, Dublin 2
Tel: (01) 662 2480 Fax: 662 8595

Head Chef: John Dunne

Alan O'Reilly's story is the most interesting Dublin restaurant tale of recent times. He was for many years the chef-patron of Clarets, in Blackrock, a solid, bourgeois place.

Then, suddenly, he changed tack.

He opened the first Morel's, above The Eagle Pub, to instant success. Hanging up his own apron, he devised simple menus, and hit lucky with a mixture of good chefs, all to stunning effect. Morel's exploded like a starburst on the south Dublin scene, its success easily explained.

Simply, it is a restaurant which truly serves its public. Everything is geared towards giving people just what they want: good food, which is familiar yet somewhat modish and modern, all at accessible prices, with a smart wine list which is amazingly inexpensive, in a deliciously hip room which is plosive with rich colours, designed by Frank Ennis.

Put these things together, and the punters turn up in their hundreds. Every night, every week

So the move into town, then, to Leeson Street and the newer Morel's Bistro, was logical. Logical, because this is a formula which bears repetition, which has the potential to go anywhere and everywhere.

But it is not a slick formula, thanks to the care and perspicacity of Morel's executive chef, John Dunne.

Mr Dunne devises and cooks, and does so with an exactitude which is mightily impressive, especially given the numbers of people he is responsible for. He has transformed his background in top-flight restaurants into an understanding of what food people truly enjoy to eat each day: dill marinated salmon with a grain mustard sauce; confit of duck leg on a pumpkin purée with roasted shallots; prawn tails with a salad of potato and French beans; blue shark on a bed of spinach; goat's cheese crostini with rocket; roast lamb with basil mash and garlic confit; classic crème brûlée; dark chocolate terrine with an espresso sauce. Terrific flavours, terrific food

The right food at the right price in the right room. It sounds so simple, but Mr O'Reilly and Mr Dunne have done it better than anyone else.

■ OPEN:
Glasthule: 6pm-10pm Mon-Sun, 12.30pm-2.30pm Sun
Leeson St: 12.30pm-2.30pm Mon-Fri, 6pm-10pm Sat

■ AVERAGE PRICE:
Lunch £11.50
Dinner £20
House Wine £10

■ CREDIT CARDS:
Visa, Access/Master, Amex, Diners

■ NOTES:
Full Licence
Children – encouraged, high chair & toys
No Wheelchair Access
The Glasthule restaurant is over the Eagle Pub, Leeson Street is in the basement of the Stephen's Hall Hotel.

101 TALBOT

Margaret Duffy & Pascal Bradley
100-102 Talbot Street
Dublin 1
Tel: (01) 874 5011 Fax: 874 5011

Head Chef: Liam Keating

If you are immune to the spell of 101 Talbot, if you are untouched by its youthful, hungry, funny, laid-back, humdinging rush, then you are almost certainly dead.

If, on the other hand, you are alive, and if you love restaurants which carve their success out against the odds, then you will, like thousands of others, adore 101.

It's set upstairs – usually a bad sign for a restaurant, but one which is becomingly increasingly meaningless – on a street which has yet to benefit from the improvements and developments which are transforming Dublin. Even an estate agent could do no better than to say of Talbot Street: "In need of some renovation".

And yet, in this unprepossessing site, Margaret Duffy and Pascal Bradley have carved out one of the best, and certainly one of the most enjoyable, Dublin restaurants.

The shock of their success can almost literally bang you about the head. Walk in here on a Wednesday lunchtime at 1.30, push back the door, and whoosh! The drive of noise and adrenaline and bonhommie which erupts at you is unique, mesmerising. You think: what on earth is going on to create such a kerfuffle and racket.

It's just people having lunch in 101. Enjoying themselves, don't you know.

No other Dublin restaurant can develop the head of steam which this place can, and when you match this with the soulful pleasure of Margaret's cooking, you understand why 101 has been such a success.

We might say of Ms Duffy's work that she is the sort of cook who prepares food which she would like to eat herself. Lamb and herb meatballs stuffed with mozzarella. Thai style blackeyed and butterbean casserole. Terrific salmon and potato fish cakes whose sweetness matches perfectly with some braised beetroot and a parsley sauce.

This is simple cooking, but it is devoted to flavour, and it never loses sight of a culinary logic which is proud and serene.

All of the other ingredients are right, of course: the smashing music; the interesting paintings which they hang in successive exhibitions, the funky staff in their t-shirts, the keenness of the prices. Put them all together and you have one of the most terrific rooms in the city.

■ OPEN:
10am-3pm Mon, 10am-11pm Tue-Sat

■ AVERAGE PRICE:
Lunch £9. Dinner from £11
House Wine from £8.95

■ CREDIT CARDS:
Visa, Access/Master, Amex, Diners

■ NOTES:
Restaurant Licence
No Wheelchair Access
Children – welcome, high chair
50 yards from O'Connell Street on the right hand side, upstairs over a camping shop.

PEACOCK ALLEY ✪

Conrad Gallagher
47 South William Street, Dublin 2
Tel: (01) 662 0760/677 0708
Fax: 671 8854

Head Chef: Conrad Gallagher

No one else cooks like Conrad Gallagher, because no no one else can cook like Conrad Gallagher.

His culinary technique is awesome, a style which seems to have been hewn out of studying the architecture of Gaudi, rather than studying in a kitchen. His food swoops and towers, climbs and ascends, as if the standard laws of gravity don't apply to Peacock Alley.

The very simplest things – the butter twisted and twirled into a turban, a bowl of soup, for heaven's sake – have been completely re-thought and revolutionised. Take the green pea soup: the bowl arrives naked except for some tomato oil and mint leaves, onto which the soup is ladled exactingly. Suddenly, a bowl of soup is no longer a food, but an event. No one else does it this way, because no one else has thought to do it this way.

This is what Mr Gallagher does: everything in Peacock Alley is spectacle. This is food as theatre, as grand guignol, as an allegory for intellectual complexity and richness, cooking as drama.

It has meant that Peacock Alley has become the most fashionable Dublin restaurant, and not just amongst those who love food. It is a dynamic space, full of adrenaline and ambition, a restaurant where you expect to be surprised, and then find the surprise is even greater than you hoped for. It is one of very few Irish restaurants which one might describe as avant garde, a place where they have constructed their own universe in counterpoint to the way others run their restaurants.

Others give you two flavours on a plate, here you will get five or six, and the brilliance lies in the balance: peppered duck breast with green risotto might have saffron mash on top of some spinach leaves in a central tower. Fillet of salmon will have a skin of couscous and pumpkin potatoes and tomato and coriander. Sea bass will have a basil mash and a clam and cockle broth with roasted peppers. The celebrated crabmeat salad will have confit lemons and coriander with marinated beetroot and a curried crème fraîche.

Thrilling. Outrageous. Unique. Of course, such complexity occasionally slips from the heights, but failures here are few and far between.

The room is delightful, the service expert, the wine list well composed and good value. Peacock Alley is one of the truly great experiences of Irish restaurant cooking.

■ **OPEN:**
12.30pm-2pm Tue-Fri
6.30pm-11pm Mon-Sat

■ **AVERAGE PRICE:**
Lunch £18.95-£26.95
Dinner from £34, £40, £45
House Wine £15

■ **CREDIT CARDS:**
Visa, Access/Master, Amex, Diners

■ **NOTES:**
Restaurant Licence
No Wheelchair Access
Children – welcome, high chair
Sth William St runs parallel to Grafton St.

POPJOYS

John Coleman & Warren Massey
4 Rathfarnham Road, Terenure
Dublin 6W
Tel: (01) 492 9346 Fax: 492 9293

Head chef: Warren Massey

In the future, the not-too-distant future, every neighbourhood will have a restaurant like Popjoys, a simple place which sits a few doors up from the crossroads at Terenure.

Thus, every neighbourhood will have a smart room where you will nevertheless feel comfortable in jeans and a jumper, and where you can also feel comfortable with your big hair and your gadabout friends on a Saturday night.

You will feel comfortable bringing the kids in for lunch, even dinner, and you will feel comfortable entertaining clients over a lazy lunch. And, of course, when it's that anniversary/birthday/family celebration, this is the place you will book.

Popjoy's is a good restaurant. It's a good restaurant not just because the cooking is good and the staff know their stuff, but because it feels right.

Warren Massey's style of cooking might be described as modern conservative. If that sounds like a contradiction, in practice it makes for scrummy food. His menu is composed almost exclusively of classic dishes – potato and watercress soup; scallops with lemon and garlic; Caesar salad; rack of lamb with confit of onion and garlic; rabbit with prunes in a pie; chicken with cabbage and bacon; skate with black butter and capers; beef with mushroom purée and fried potatoes.

These combinations are tried and trusted, and Mr Massey then makes sure he gets them right: expert Caesar salad; fried goat's cheese with a roasted red pepper dressing is precise; fillet of beef a definition of what the dish should be about – punchy flavours which coalesce to make something amiably comforting, and desserts are absolutely knockout.

While all this is going on on the plate, John Coleman applies similar expertise to the front of house. He can manage to pour you a glass of wine while en route to clearing a table, just before he shakes hands with a punter and takes a booking over the phone for seventeen for Thursday week. Greeting, meeting, orchestrating, all these acts are subsumed into a meticulous ballet which you immediately take for granted.

Local folk, in the local place, having one hell of a good time, all of them comfortable as could be. Every neighbourhood needs a place like this, and every neighbourhood should have one.

■ OPEN:
12.30pm-2.30pm Tue-Fri, 6.30pm-10.30pm Tue-Sat, 12.30pm-3.30pm Sun

■ AVERAGE PRICE:
Lunch £11.95 + 10%
Dinner from £18 + 10%
House Wine from £8.50 + 10%

■ CREDIT CARDS:
Visa, Access/Master, Amex, Diners

■ NOTES:
Restaurant Licence
Wheelchair Access, but not to toilets
Children – welcome if well behaved
Terenure Cross Roads

THE RAJDOOT TANDOORI

Ricky Singh
26-28 Clarendon Street, Dublin 2
Tel: (01) 679 4274 Fax: 679 4274

Head Chef: Krishan Kumar Dangol

The Rajdoot has become a staple of restaurant life in Dublin, a place so well cemented in the eating fabric of the city that one cannot imagine having to live without its promise of superb ethnic food.

It has achieved this position amongst the pre-eminent Indian restaurants not just by its search for authenticity, but also by virtue of a terrific level of consistency since it opened.

Scan back over the years, scan back over the visits made during those years to the Rajdoot, and what one remembers is not just the satisfaction which this robust Moghul cuisine delivers, but above all the fact that, on each and every occasion, each and every dish was instinctively, reliably good.

One is glad, then, that the menu is so extensive, allowing forays into different tastes on each occasion.

Visit with a vegetarian friend, and one can seize on the torchy delights of charcoal-grilled Vegetable Shashlik, the paneer cheese cooked into soft succulence, the capsicums and tomatoes all smoky and gorgeous. Complement this with Channa Bunna, moist chick peas coated in a viscous, yielding sauce, a fluffy Vegetable Biryani which is served with a darkly coloured and flavoured dish of lentils, or choose to mop up the food with your fingers, and order Onion Kulcha, with the lovely flat tablets of bread enlivened with onions and herbs.

Each dish is perfectly realised, the tandoori specialities all bright orange and vividly flavoured, the meat and seafood dishes fulsome, rib-sticking melds of cream, nuts, butter and herbs, the breads and rices delicate, appropriate, blissful.

Another visit might feature their speciality of duck tikka, a little touch of honey giving a sweet finish to the meat, and the superb saag paneeer, with their own cottage cheese perfectly melding with spinach. Lamb badami, in its creamy almond and pistachio sauce, is mellow, whilst some chicken jalfrezi is richly garlicky.

This is excellent cooking but, just sometimes, one wishes that the Rajdoot would loosen up a little bit, and let some of the dishes become a little wilder, a little less serene. Other Indian restaurants in Dublin are now seeing this as the way ahead, as people seek ever more authentic tastes. It is time for the Rajdoot, which has traditionally led the way for many years, to follow suit.

■ OPEN:
1pm-2.30pm, 7.30pm-10pm Mon-Sun
■ AVERAGE PRICE:
Lunch £6.95
Dinner from £15.50-£19.50
House Wine from £9.50
■ CREDIT CARDS:
Visa, Access/Master, Amex, Diners

■ NOTES:
Full Pub Licence
Wheelchair Access
Children – welcome, high chair
Part of the Westbury Hotel complex.

RED BANK

Terry McCoy
7 Church Street, Skerries
Co Dublin
Tel: (01) 849 1005 Fax: 849 1598
e-mail: redbank@iol.ie

Head Chef: Terry McCoy

He is, by this stage, one of the senior statesmen of Irish Cooking, is Terry McCoy, and his Red Bank restaurant is one of the most respected and long-established in the country.

So you might take the trip out to Skerries and imagine you will meet some portly chap, with a few threads of hair, a big ego, and a cosy bank balance, and little to achieve.

Not a bit of it. Mr McCoy has a mane of hair in a pony tail, so much energy it almost makes you feel tired, and an inexhaustible hunger for a challenge. We don't know what his bank balance is like, but chances are, as he has just developed some rooms in the Red Bank Lodge near to the restaurant, that he has just spent it all.

He was one of the finalists in the first An Bord Bia competition, is forever winning awards for his fish cookery, and as we write this book he will be heading off to France to represent Ireland in the Bocuse d'Or competition. He likes a challenge.

Mr McCoy is a confident competition person because he can cook. Indeed, when it comes to fish cookery, he is as talented as any other panhandler in the country. In his own words, he aims to treat his food "with respect and with sympathy", virtues that are immediately evident in both the appearance and, especially, the taste of his food. Terry McCoy understands the virtue of simplicity, and yet still loves to indulge himself in unlikely elaborations, which he achieves successfully.

Indeed, some of the pairings of fish and unexpected and unlikely stuffings and spices, show a very deep understanding of this desired mix of respect and sympathy: barbecued salmon with a peanut butter sauce; won ton dumplings of seafood in a salad; Kenure house hake, where the brilliantly white fish is stuffed with horseradish; haddock with Creole spices; wings of skate with spring onions. Allowing this playfulness a free hand also contributes a lovely variety of textures.

Abetting this skill is McCoy's proud and devoted sourcing of foods from his region. Flour from the White River Mill in Dunleer, salmon from the Forman family, leeks from North County Dublin farmers, oysters from Carlingford, fish and shellfish landed at Skerries itself. This pride in the quality of local foods is charming, and gives a deserved sense of importance and confidence to the Red Bank.

■ OPEN:
7pm-9.30pm Tue-Sat, 12.30pm-2.15pm Sun
■ AVERAGE PRICE:
Lunch £15.75. Dinner from £23-£25
House Wine from £11
■ CREDIT CARDS:
Visa, Access/Master, Amex, Diners

■ NOTES:
Restaurant Licence
Wheelchair Access
Children – over 10 yrs welcome
Skerries is 29km north of Dublin.

ROLY'S BISTRO

Roly Saul & Colin O'Daly
7 Ballsbridge Terrace
Ballsbridge, Dublin 4
Tel: (01) 668 2611 Fax: 660 8535

Head Chef: Colin O'Daly

The greatest success story in recent Irish restaurant history, Roly Saul's Bistro is essentially the prototype for the new neighbourhood restaurant.

A combination of excellent food at excellent prices, with excellent service in a darling room, it is the very summation of what a local restaurant should aim for, and Roly's achieves the ideal with gas in the tank.

Although somewhat grand, it is never pretentious, and the dedication to service – to making sure that people get what they want, and thereby have the great time they want – is inspiring.

And like any other great success story, it broke the mould. Roly Saul used to run a little neighbourhood place in Dun Laoghaire. Colin O'Daly, his chef, was a product of the grand school of cuisine, the fiddly, expensive stuff. They seemed like the classic Odd Couple, doomed to discord. But, the two came together to form Roly's and, kaboom! we have liftoff!

Of course they were fortunate to open at a time when the Dublin economy was improving, but they couldn't have known that. Like the opening of Belfast's Roscoff, in 1989, Roly's worked because it was answering the need, amongst people who love restaurants, for smart cooking in a smart place which did not burst the bank. Roly's is as grand as anywhere, but its prices are those of a bistro. Vitally, whilst it attracts a business crowd at lunchtime, it also pulls in the locals in the evenings: it is a neighbourhood place.

Colin O'Daly oversees the food with a genial, driven nature that strives to get everything as good as it can be: fillet of pork with oyster mushrooms and Madeira; venison pie with cranberries; roast leg of lamb with potato gratin; salmon with vanilla; smoked fish cakes; classic desserts.

Of course, given the numbers they do, there are times when the food slips from its normally impressive heights. Ideally this would never happen, but it is easy to forgive because there is never a moment of cynicism about the place. If they got lazy and didn't care, you might be annoyed. If you felt that they were sitting back on their laurels and just packing them in, then you might be miffed. But they do care, and nothing is taken for granted.

■ **OPEN:**
Noon-3pm Mon-Sun, 6pm-10pm Sun-Thur, 6pm-10.30pm Fri & Sat

■ **AVERAGE PRICE:**
Lunch £10.50 + 10%
Dinner £15-£20
House Wine from £8.95

■ **CREDIT CARDS:**
Visa, Access/Master, Amex, Diners

■ **NOTES:**
Restaurant Licence
Wheelchair Access
Children – welcome, high chair
On the corner between Ballsbridge and Herbert Park.

SAAGAR

Nisheeth Tak
16 Harcourt Street
Dublin 2
Tel: (01) 475 5060/475 5012

Head Chef: Vivek Sehni

A friend who visited Saagar described the impact of the restaurant's cooking, and the service of the manager Nisheeth Tak, as creating "an emphasis that is very clearly on your enjoyment and pleasure".

Enjoyment, and pleasure. That's Saagar. You feel welcome, you feel set up to have a good time, from the second Mr Tak shows you to your table in the low-lit square room with its ululating music and respectfully formal ambience.

It is no surprise, however, that an air of confidence and control should be so evident in Saagar, for the restaurant is the sister to Mullingar's much-respected Little India, which Saagar's owners, Sunil and Meera Kumar, have run since 1992.

Their success has been founded on a expert appreciation of true Indian cooking. "We don't believe in serving European versions of Indian dishes", Sunil Kumar says. "We stick to the original recipes and we present the complete range of regional dishes and cooking styles that makes Indian cuisine unique".

This is an imprimatur which the restaurant executes with aplomb. Indeed, Saagar not only cooks authentic Indian food, but also offers a selection of original dishes, described on the menu as "Chef's Favourite".

These can be creations such as Murg Mussallam – chicken stuffed with minced lamb, rice and egg, and flavoured with saffron – and Lamb Aatish – lamb marinated with spices and cooked in a cognac flavoured sauce – with one of the finest their Murgh Dumpukht, announced as "Our chef's own creation based on a secret recipe".

This is a sensation, with the chicken strongly flavoured with almonds which give a sensuously lush and velvety texture, the sweetness of the dish enhanced by coconut. It hides under a little pastry hat, the dough somewhat along the style of a chapatti-meets-samosa confection, yet unlike either of those.

Fire-eaters will enjoy the fine lamb vindaloo, or maybe a Goan prawn curry – dishes from Goa and Hyderabad are specialities of the restaurant – but the precision of flavours is evident everywhere.

The fact that Saagar is such wonderful value for money, and the serene ambience of the room means that one wants to head back soonest, for this taste of the real thing.

■ OPEN:
12.30pm-3pm Mon-Fri
6pm-11.30pm Mon-Sun
■ AVERAGE PRICE:
Lunch £8
Dinner from £16
House Wine from £10
■ CREDIT CARDS:
Visa, Access/Master, Amex, Diners

■ NOTES:
Wine Licence
Wheelchair Access. Children – welcome
Harcourt Street runs off St Stephen's Green. The restaurant is in the basement.

THE TEA ROOMS

Bono, Edge, Harry Crosbie
The Clarence Hotel
6-8 Wellington Quay, Dublin 2
Tel: (01) 670 9000 Fax: 670 7800

Head Chef: Michael Martin

It says a lot about Michael Martin that even during the lengthy hiatus when the Clarence was being refurbished, he held on waiting for the time when it would open again, and he could show his style.

It also says a lot about him that that style – contemporary, filled with modern notes, and yet fundamentally simple – should have taken him some time to perfect once the doors of the Tea Room were open again.

What it says about him is that he is not a slick operator, someone who can churn out food which is merely proficient. Indeed, in the early days there certainly seemed to be a tension between a restaurant which wanted to be cool and cosmopolitan, and a chef who wanted to be rootsy. The food was almost frightened to be flavourful.

But Mr Martin soon settled that, and in this gorgeous space he is now all set to achieve great things.

The menu leans heavily towards satisfying a diverse clientele; the high rollers from the hotel who want to see foie gras and lobster on the menu, and the ordinary decent citizens of Dublin who are likely to stroll in at lunch or dinnertime.

There are thus no fewer than ten starters – smoked chicken, spring onion and potato pie with puy lentils; the soufflé of Swiss cheeses roasted in cream; soups such as Thai coconut soup, consommé of wild mushroom and tarragon, red mullet, and usually eleven main courses – corn-fed chicken with new potatoes and leeks and a morel and tarragon cream; risotto of cepes; fillet of lamb with spiced couscous; steamed cod with aubergine blinis.

This is quintessential modern cooking, anxious about fat content, careful to include all the modern elements and ingredients, but when they get things right there can be memorable, distinctive flavours.

The size and diversity of the menu puts quite a lot of pressure on the kitchen, but Michael Martin has buckled the focus of the cooking into his style, and the food is proud to be individual.

The room itself is gorgeous, and service is professional. The wine list, however, needs more notes and descriptions of the wines, which are a good selection, albeit expensive.

Mr Martin held on for a long time waiting for the Tea Rooms, because he felt this was the place to achieve his dreams. It looks like he was right.

■ OPEN:
12.30pm-2.30pm Mon-Fri, 6.30pm-10.30pm Mon-Sat, 6.30pm-10pm Sun

■ AVERAGE PRICE:
Lunch from £13,50
Dinner from £17.50
House Wine from £10

■ CREDIT CARDS:
Visa, Access/Master, Amex, Diners

■ NOTES:
Restaurant Licence
Full Wheelchair Access
Children – welcome, high chair
In the Clarence Hotel, on the Liffey.

THORNTON'S ✪

Kevin Thornton
1 Portobello Road, Dublin 8
Tel: (01) 454 9067 Fax: 453 2947
e-mail: thorntons@iol.ie

Head Chef: Kevin Thornton

Maybe it's because modern cooking has become so fragmented that the sense of pure culinary devotion which we find in the cooking of Kevin Thornton, is so impressive, so memorable.

Both technically skilled and vibrantly effective, Mr Thornton's work is also admirably pure. Dedicated and devoted, it is designed to achieve the very best that can be done with the ingredients to hand, and the skill of those hands. It reminds you that here is a cook whose work is never self-serving, a man whose craft operates outside any modish consideration of fashion or ego. It reminds you that, for Kevin Thornton, the business of cooking is a vocation.

His style is almost completely abstract, searching out alliances and allegiances of flavours amongst ingredients and then placing them together on a plate. A little amuse of roasted scallop with an earthy coin of black truffle and a slurp of truffle oil shows this urgent search for harmony, and yet, like a fine piece of music, it is something which is at once totally involving and, yet, completely abstract, devoted to itself.

Mr Thornton will thus pair fillets of brill and red mullet with olives and red pepper to jigsaw their respective flavours, pair a tartlet of mallard duck with a quince jus for relishful resonance, sharpen the flavour of asparagus and artichoke in a salad by using a walnut vinaigrette, with each dish offering extra echoes of the principal flavours. He has long since left behind the complexity which his early work overindulged in, honing his skills to the point where there is nothing superfluous in a dish. There is an almost organic sense of completeness to his work these days.

This dedication to creating perfect symmetries, to finding the key flavour elements in a dish, has ushered in a commendable maturity in Kevin Thornton's cooking. Simple dishes such as magret of duck with chestnuts, turnip and pommes purée are done perfectly, his fish cookery likewise has become a showcase for flavour, as in a fillet of seabass with a tomato and basil tartlet

The peripherals of the restaurant are splendid – the upstairs dining room lean and bright, the music splendid, the breads magnificent, and the service could not be better. Thornton's is a shrine to the muse of the kitchen.

■ **OPEN:**
6.30pm-10.30pm Tue-Sat, & Fri lunch
■ **AVERAGE PRICE:**
Lunch £15.50. Dinner from £23.50
House Wine from £10.15
■ **CREDIT CARDS:**
Visa, Access/Master, Amex, Diners

■ **NOTES:**
Full Pub Licence
Wheelchair Access
Children – welcome, high chair
On the Grand Canal, between the Rathmines and Harold's X bridges.

DESTRY'S

Patrick & Julia Foyle
Main Street, Clifden, Co Galway
Tel: (095) 21722 Fax: 21608

Head Chef: Dermot Gannon

Some Irish chefs write menus which are more thrilling to read than the climax of a good Elmore Leonard thriller, and Dermot Gannon is one of those chefs.

Timbale of smoked lamb, quail eggs and Parmesan, garlic and horseradish cream.

Thai spiced crab and shrimp chowder.

Millefeuille of crab and spinach with an apricot and apple chutney.

Pan-seared scallops with spinach tortellini poached in a citrus cream.

Breast of guinea hen stuffed with sun-dried banana on a grilled vegetable, fagioli bean and parmesan moussaka.

Roast monkfish wrapped in a smoked lamb crust with avocado and almond salsa.

Honey, is this drool territory, or what?

But there's more. Mr Gannon can not only dream, devise and write it, he can cook it. Here is a chef who can make it taste even better than it sounds.

Paddy Foyle, who owns Destry's and the nearby Quay House, was the man who gave Dermot Gannon his break in the kitchen. It's fun to talk to Mr Foyle and hear him attempt to explain Mr Gannon's wizardry.

He tries, but he can't for the life of him explain the instinctive completeness and the endless inventiveness which this local fellow can come up with in the kitchen. "He's an alchemist", says Paddy Foyle, lost in admiration, shaking his head in wonder. "An alchemist!".

It's true that Dermot Gannon can change base materials into culinary magnificence. The audaciousness of wrapping some monkfish in smoked lamb. The splash of raspberry vinegar in the cabbage stewed with garlic and smoked bacon which accompanies some venison. The luxurious stuffing of smoked salmon, goat's cheese and shrimp which he uses to stuff roasted peppers. The couscous and sesame crust which envelopes field mushrooms stuffed with ricotta, garlic and herbs. The sun-dried banana with the guinea hen. How does he dream this stuff up?

Mr Gannon is lucky to be able to produce this funky, fizzing cooking in a funky, fizzing restaurant. Destry's is a smashing space – loose, limber, lively, lovely, youthful – the perfect restaurant for the vivacious town of Clifden.

The combination of the two is irresistible, and thrilling.

Alchemy, indeed.

■ OPEN:
Noon-3pm, 6pm-10pm Mon-Sat
■ AVERAGE PRICE:
Lunch from £7.50
Dinner from £15
House Wine from £10.95
■ CREDIT CARDS:
Visa, Access

■ NOTES:
Wine Licence
Wheelchair Access
Children – welcome if supervised
On the main street in the town centre.

DRIMCONG HOUSE ✪

Gerry & Marie Galvin
Moycullen, Co Galway
Tel: (091) 555115/555585
Fax: 555836

Head Chef: Gerry Galvin

It may very well be the case that when we cast our minds back, at the century's end, and wonder just who amongst all of the Irish chefs has exerted the most persuasive influence for the good of Irish cooking, that we will decide that Gerry Galvin has been the individual who has achieved the most.

He has taught the younger generation of cooks who have passed through his kitchens to treat food with care and respect, and to respect themselves.

His annual classes have opened the eyes of countless amateur cooks to the magic and the thrill of cooking.

His book, "The Drimcong Food Affair", is the most erudite and admirable work about the business of running an Irish restaurant ever written by an Irish cook.

And his true glory, the restaurant which is Drimcong House, just outside Moycullen in County Galway, stands as testament to a man whose vision of a functioning restaurant is broader, more intellectually resolved, and more complete than perhaps any other Irish restaurateur.

Consider the facts. A man with no formal training in professional kitchens, Mr Galvin has long pioneered the idea that a restaurant is someplace where children should be catered for, seriously. He has always had special, intelligent, menus for vegetarians, years before anyone else thought of it.

His prices have always been keen, which means his restaurant is accessible to all – Gerry Galvin long ago realised the intellectual and creative death which is implicit in running a pricey place for rich folks.

And, with all of this, Mr Galvin has produced delicious food, food with personality, food with a sense of culture, food with a sense of history, food which is eloquently expressive of what we mean when we talk about a "food culture".

Eel and pike mousse with horseradish and dill creams and salad; grilled oysters and smoked salmon gratin; pork steak with crispy risotto à la crème; slow-cooked ox cheek with oysters, bacon and lovage; fillet of lamb with a summer salad. Darling food, darling cooking.

With his wife, Marie, Gerry Galvin has created in Drimcong one of the great Irish restaurants, a place which stands as testament to generosity, intelligence, and the culture of cooking.

■ OPEN:
6.30pm-10.30pm Tue-Sat (closed from Xmas to March)

■ AVERAGE PRICE:
Dinner from £25. House Wine from £11.50

■ CREDIT CARDS:
Visa, Access/Master, Amex, Diners

■ NOTES:
Restaurant Licence
Wheelchair Access
Children – welcome, special menu £10
9 miles west of Galway on the Clifden Road, just beyond Moycullen village.

ERRISEASK HOUSE HOTEL ✪

Stefan & Christian Matz
Ballyconeely, Connemara
Co Galway
Tel: (095) 23553 Fax: 23639

Head Chef: Stefan Matz

They are a couple of shy, quiet young men, Christian and Stefan Matz, diffident about their skills, modest about their ambitions, which makes the fact that dinner in the Erriseaske is one of the most thrilling dramas in Irish food an even greater delight.

Little prepares you to be knocked sideways by Stefan Matz's cooking. There is nothing grandiose about the restaurant or the menu, there is little about the house – a small, shore-side hotel – which leads you to expect the fireworks which will turn up on the plate. But, turn up they will: this is extraordinary cooking, a starburst of culinary brilliance.

To try to understand the complexity of his work would require an entire chapter, but every dish, every course, will have a little secret buried in its composition, a little complexity, a little cleverness.

The home-made gravadlax will be cured in a mixture of Swedish vinegar and sugar; in the lobster salad the sweet shellfish will have been marinated in a chervil vinegar; a slender ravioli stuffed with a mixture of lobster and mushrooms has a trump card in the use of a little consommé in its salad dressing.

He makes an incredibly time-consuming clear tomato soup, which must be eaten the day it is made, and will depth-charge the flavour with a tiny ravioli filled with a veal and herb stuffing, doing something similar with a cream of watercress soup whose dapper greenness is undercut by a julienne of fish.

With main courses, a quartet of raviolis will have a sauce which is a balmy meld of white wine, shallots, cream and lemon juice, but again the need for a bass note in a float-away dish will come from using some port and madeira. Those same boozes will, amazingly, be perfectly matched to a loin of veal with two sauces, the second sauce a light foie gras.

The cheeseboard in The Erriseaske sets Irish farmhouse cheeses in competition with their French counterparts, on a board arranged from sweet cheeses through to strongly flavoured ones, another indication of how everything here is a game with flavour, another chance to make magic, to present the challenge of discovery. Desserts, such as the celebrated lemon tart, are melting, crumbling pieces of perfection.

So, expect the unexpected. Above all, expect to be amazed.

■ OPEN:
1pm-2pm Fri-Sat, 6.30pm-9pm Mon-Sun (Wed residents only)

■ AVERAGE PRICE:
Lunch £14.90. Dinner from £23.50-£32.50
House Wine from £11

■ CREDIT CARDS:
Visa, Access/Master, Amex, Diners

■ NOTES:
Restaurant Licence
Wheelchair Access, but not to toilets
Children – welcome, high chair
Take the coast road from Clifden to Ballyconeely, then follow the signposts.

HIGH MOORS

Hugh & Eileen Griffin
Dooneen, Clifden, Co Galway
Tel: (095) 21342

Head Chef: Eileen Griffin

Let's talk about that certain place, that certain restaurant, which is just the sort of place you dream of discovering when you are on holiday, all carefree and keen-as-mustard.

You would like to find someplace where the food had something of a domestic character, indeed where the restaurant itself had a domestic character, almost as if someone was welcoming you into their home.

And you would hope that the food would be simply cooked, inexpensive, quietly expressive of its own tastes and flavours, local, distinctive, food which speaks of its place.

And you would hope the service would be serene and calm, creating a bright, happy atmosphere, for you want, really, a night which begins slowly but, then, gradually, takes off, until soon it is sometime in the small hours and that voice you are hearing in that pub singing that song is... well, your voice, actually.

High Moors is the place you want to find, the place where you kick off an evening like this, the place which is perfect for your holiday special. It opens at Easter, closes in the autumn, and in between Hugh and Eileen Griffin welcome people into a restaurant which is, in fact, their home.

You can look out across the wild, remorseless moors from their sitting room, as sunset falls, and await the quiet pleasures of Eileen Griffin's fine cooking, served by Hugh and a gaggle of local girls.

It will be simple food but it will taste delicious because a lot of it will have been grown by Hugh himself, just a stone's throw down the road. As you drove up to the restaurant, you will have driven past the field where many of the vegetables which will appear tonight on your plate were grown.

The rest of the ingredients will have been sourced locally, and Eileen knows how to get the best out of them: lovely home-smoked chicken with an orange and honey sauce; confit of duck with a walnut-dressed salad; brill with a chervil hollandaise; breast of duck with apple, sage and potato purée.

With half a dozen Cleggan oysters to begin, and some summer berries and currants in a brandy syrup to conclude, and a few bottles from their nifty little list, you will smile and say that you have found that place you were thinking of, that certain holiday restaurant you dreamed about. Hugh and Eileen and High Moors just made your holiday wish come true.

■ **OPEN:**
6.30pm-9.30pm Wed-Sun
■ **AVERAGE PRICE:**
Dinner from £12.90
House Wine from £8.90
■ **CREDIT CARDS:**
Visa, Access/Master, Amex
■ **NOTES:**
Wine Licence
Wheelchair Access
Children – welcome, high chair
1km from Clifden, side road signposted on Ballyconneely road, 50m from town.

GALWAY

KIRWAN'S LANE CREATIVE CUISINE

Michael O'Grady
Kirwan's Lane, Galway
Tel: (091) 568266

Head Chef: Hubert Muhlbadher

Kirwan's Lane is a classic modern restaurant, a long, lean room with rag-painted walls, subdued lighting, an open kitchen, and a menu littered with all the modern menu notes: parsnip shavings, basil batter, lemongrass, even the awful affectation which means that they call coriander by its American title, cilantro.

It is owned by Michael O'Grady, whose family have run the long-established O'Grady's Restaurant, in Clifden, for decades. Mr O'Grady, in moving into the city, has moved smack into the modern world, bravely adding the sub-title "Creative Cuisine" to the restaurant's name.

Look at the menu and you might think that being creative in a modern kitchen just means mucking about with the classics, for in Kirwan's Lane they have a salad which includes smoked mussels and they call it a "Caesar Salad".

Caesar Salad doesn't have smoked mussels. Nor does it have thin slices of red pepper, as theirs does. And you don't make it with iceberg lettuce, as they had done. And you certainly don't make it with smoked chicken, as they include in another version of their "Caesar Salad".

So, does Kirwan's Lane's creative cuisine amount to any more than messing around with menu-speak? Well, it does, actually. What they are best at is, ironically, the great bistro staples. A dish of homemade sausages with sauerkraut and mash, the latter artfully smashed in the modern style, is good: simple, enjoyable food which the kitchen accomplishes well.

Lamb's liver with an onion confit and corn and potato cakes also shows just how good they are at this punchy, spoonsome style of cooking.

But if they can do the bistro stuff perfectly, they can do the nursery puddings to perfection. A clever apple brulée – the apple baked and then topped with a seared caramelised hat, is excellent fun, whilst a generous bowl of rice pudding with raspberry jam lacks only a smidgin of extra vanilla to make it really memorable.

The service in Kirwan's Lane is good, the wine list needs work to make it interesting, but anyone who plays to their strengths, and chooses snappy, flavourful dishes, will find enjoyable cooking, just the sort of hunger-satisfying food you want in a hungry city like Galway.

■ OPEN:
Noon-12.30pm, 6pm-10.15pm Mon-Sat
■ AVERAGE PRICE:
Lunch £12.50
Dinner from £23
House Wine from £10.95
■ CREDIT CARDS:
Visa, Access/Master, Amex

■ NOTES:
Wine Licence
No Wheelchair Access
Children – over 8 yrs welcome
Kirwan's Lane runs off the bottom end of Quay Street.

ALLO'S ➔

Armel Whyte & Helen Mullane
Listowel, Co Kerry
Tel: (068) 22880

Head Chef: Armel Whyte

With everything they do in the food business, Helen and Armel create an archetype, a gleaming, glistening slice of originality. When they ran Loaves & Fishes, down on the Ring of Kerry, they created the perfect holiday restaurant – romantic, entrancing, away-from-it-all.

Since they made the move to Listowel, and opened Allo's Bistro in this most beautiful bar, they have met with amazing success. Once again, they have created the archetype, the perfect bistro cooking in the perfect bar. Allo's is the Irish country town pub of your dreams.

They are successful because their combination of talents means that their ventures offer all you want. If there is a better front-of-house person than Ms Mullane, we must confess that we have yet to come across them. Disciplined, loquacious, amusing, she knows exactly how to read a customer, and a customer's needs. A smart government would hire Ms Mullane to teach her skills to everyone in the people business.

Mr Whyte completes this dynamic double-act by rattling his pots and pans in an inimitable way. His cuisine has become more distinctive and authoritative in recent years as he has gained in both experience and confidence. He now produces some of the loveliest food you will find anywhere, lovely flavours, lovely tastes, lovely textures.

He will pair grilled duck livers with spiced prunes and couscous, and create a salad with a confit of pheasant and a raspberry vinaigrette. These dishes show his style: sharp, well-defined tastes are used to complement perfectly cooked staples, so there will be a crisply refreshing lime beurre blanc with some panfried scallops, or a tart berry sauce with the amazing local ducks reared by Mrs Murphy – these should not be missed: Mary Murphy's ducks ooze flavour.

But Mr Whyte also knows when to leave well alone: his grilled sole on the bone is meticulous, his chargrilled fillet of beef with a pink peppercorn and cream sauce is sublime. In its own quiet, proud way, this cooking cannot be bettered.

But Helen and Armel will surely attempt to better it in the future. They are not people to sit still, even when something is as successful as Allo's, so keep a close eye on future developments. They are people who always want to create archetypes anew.

■ OPEN:
Noon-7pm Mon-Sat.
Dinner served 7pm-8.15pm Tue-Sat.
No dinner Feb. Reservation essential

■ AVERAGE PRICE:
Lunch £5-£9. Dinner from £22
House Wine from £9.95

■ CREDIT CARDS:
Visa, Access/Master

■ NOTES:
Full Pub Licence
Wheelchair Access
Children – welcome, high chair
Centre of Listowel, opposite Garda station.

BEGINISH RESTAURANT

Pat & John Moore
Green Street, Dingle, Co Kerry
Tel: (066) 51588 Fax: 51591

Head Chef: Pat Moore

Pat Moore loves to cook the classics, and there are few who can cook them better than Mrs Moore and her team.

Just look at the Beginish menu, and its respectful roll call of the great dishes.

Smoked wild salmon with horseradish cream; tomato and goat's cheese mousse with fennel; Cromane mussels with beurre blanc; sole on the bone meuniere; smoked haddock and parsley sauce; fillet of beef with pepper sauce and rosti; fillet of turbot with olive oil scented potato purée and white wine sauce; sticky toffee pudding; crème brûlée; rhubarb soufflé tart.

Timeless, elegant, perfect. And that is what the Beginish is all about.

Mrs Moore is a keen student of the culinary fashions, forever poring over books to see what so-and-so is up to, or what influences are all the rage in London or Paris.

But, truth be told, her heart lies with the classics, and it does so because she loves the elegance of these dishes, their sense of completeness and their formality. Her search in the kitchen, then, is to achieve these dishes perfectly.

And she can do it.

Don't imagine, however, that just because they do the classics that Beginish is some sort of soulless machine. Anything but. It is stylish and creative, exactly the sort of restaurant you want to find in Dingle, but fear you might not.

Pat and John Moore could sidle by by churning stuff out for tourists, as many others in the town do. But they won't allow themselves to do that. They can't.

They can't because they chase the goddess of perfection in every dish they make. Simple things in here can be so precisely, confidently, exactingly executed that they leave you speechless with admiration: a white crab meat salad which is majestic; a salad of mixed greens with toasted pine kernels and a blue cheese dressing; loin of spring lamb with rosemary; some grilled wild salmon with a leek fondue; that incredible concoction which is the rhubarb soufflée tart with a crème anglaise.

To do this right takes commitment, and a vision of what a serious restaurant should aspire to. All the essential details are properly seen to – breads, service, wines, decor, ambience – and in a town where others are happy to produce fodder for tourists, the discipline of the Beginish is inspiring.

■ OPEN:
6pm-10pm Tue-Sun

■ AVERAGE PRICE:
Dinner from £20
House Wine from £11.50

■ CREDIT CARDS:
Visa, Access/Master, Amex, Diners

■ NOTES:
Full Pub Licence
No Wheelchair Access
Children – welcome
Just below the Green Street Church, on the other side of the street.

D'ARCY'S

Matthew & Aileen d'Arcy
Main Street, Kenmare
Co Kerry
Tel: (064) 41589 Fax: 41589

Head Chef: Matthew d'Arcy

Matt d'Arcy is a restaurateur on a roll.

Since moving to this informal restaurant on Main Street, his cooking has just got better and better.

"Flawless technique and understated flavours", were the essentials of his style, the "New York Times" decided, some years back. Perhaps more accurately, they said, "Some of Mr d'Arcy's combinations are daring". Indeed they are.

The last time we ate here, pooped after a hard day's work, Mr d'Arcy's cooking woke us from our fatigue by virtue of its terrific flavoursomeness. He has always been a great kitchen technician, with a dazzling technique at his disposal, but over the years his food has found a drop-dead gorgeousness which is utterly invigorating and inviting.

His love of variation and complication, of finding new alliances, is rampant throughout an agonising-to-choose-from menu: warm ravioli of prawn mousse with a sweet pepper scented butter; salmon with noodles in a light curry sauce; chicken and noodle soup with star anise; scallops fried in the pan with leeks and grapes; prawn tails on a bed of ratatouille; escalope of veal with capers and butter.

This is smashing food, from a chef whose work seems to have gotten more youthful as the years go by.

He has become more daring, and more inventive, with an energy enervating all of his work. It makes Mr d'Arcy's dishes endlessly fascinating.

At the same time as one relishes the inventiveness and unexpectedness, you are also struck by the fact that this cooking, with its impressive architecture of design and concentrated focus of taste, manages to be both classic and, at the same time, very modern.

Such intelligent striding across the barriers of taste and the styles of time demands a singular discipline. Matt d'Arcy has it.

As Mr d'Arcy has developed into a more confident cook, his staff have grown in confidence also, making the business of dinner in d'Arcy's a joy.

The dining room is a simple, enjoyable space, perhaps at its best on cool evenings when the fire burns bright, and there is a good bottle of wine to enjoy with this good food, but also charming on a sunny summer evening, when this most wonderful town seems to be out there waiting for you.

■ OPEN:
6pm-11pm Mon-Sun (Apr-Oct), 7pm-10.30pm Fri-Sun (Oct-Mar)
■ AVERAGE PRICE:
Dinner from £20
House Wine from £10
■ CREDIT CARDS:
Visa, Access/Master

■ NOTES:
Wine Licence
Wheelchair Access
Children – welcome, half portions
At the top end of Main Street, on the left hand side as you drive up the hill.

GABY'S SEAFOOD RESTAURANT

Geert & Marie Maes
17 High Street
Killarney, Co Kerry
Tel: (064) 32519 Fax: 32747

Head Chef: Geert Maes

Gaby's is just the sort of restaurant you want and hope to find yourself in, when your best holiday mood is under threat from the blarneyed bluff of the bogus town of Killarney.

The signature sign of Gaby's – an upturned corrach being carried by three men across the strand – has stayed the same over the twenty years since Geert and Marie Maes have been here, and so, over the years, has the consistency and effectiveness of Mr Maes' cooking.

In a town full of froth and flotsam, and endless menus packed with ersatz food, Mr Maes is a serious cook, a member of the Eurotoques association and a man who relishes pitching his skills into competitions.

Above all, he is a chef who knows very well what he does best, and this professionalism means that Gaby's is just the sort of restaurant you desperately need in Killarney, especially on one of those days when the streets are clogged with human traffic, and you clamour for respite, and for something true, accomplished, and delicious.

The restaurant is almost a café in style, with a small bar near the door, a garden at the back, and inside it is cleverly arranged on different levels, the total exuding an easy-going, bare-boarded, European feel.

The cooking, obviously, concentrates on Mr Maes' strength with fish and shellfish, with many of the dishes offered being served cold, and the others served hot. There are of course good oysters, smoked salmon, and a fine shellfish platter, whilst the hot dishes might include black sole in a cream sauce; hot salmon or hot smoked trout, and their own secret way of preparing lobster, fresh from the tank.

Gaby's is a place which manages to feel just right for an informal lunch - when they offer soups and sandwiches – and yet it has the right sort of formality and ambience also for both a family meal with a big crowd of folk, or a romantic dinner.

Gaby's is a real and welcome antidote to the Disneyland surrealism which accounts for much of Killarney. It is reassuring, also, to note that the availability of dishes is always subject to the success, or lack of success, of the local fleets.

So, press hands together and pray for good weather.

■ OPEN:
12.30pm-2.30pm Tue-Sat
6pm-10pm Mon-Sat

■ AVERAGE PRICE:
Lunch £9
Dinner from £20
House Wine from £10

■ CREDIT CARDS:
Visa, Access/Master, Amex, Diners

■ NOTES:
Restaurant Licence
Wheelchair Access
Children – welcome, high chair
Killarney town centre, on the right hand side of the street which takes you out west. Look for the famous sign.

PACKIES

Tom & Maura Foley O'Connell
Henry Street, Kenmare, Co Kerry
Tel: (064) 41508 Fax: 42135

Head Chef: Maura Foley

Maura Foley's cooking renders criticism, and critics, redundant

She cooks wonderful food. She cooks it in a wonderfully original style, which she has honed over a couple of decades at the stove. She sources her foods – and above all her wonderful fish – from the finest suppliers.

She cooks this food and serves it in a simple, lovely, wonderfully inviting room. She employs excellent staff who suit the place perfectly. Her prices are not merely fair, but wonderfully cheap. She has assembled a fine, suitable wine list. She does all of this wonderfully, modestly, without any egotism, with maternal care.

So, what is the critical summation after a dinner in Packie's? A dinner of crab salad with lemongrass and coconut dressing, then fillet of salmon with an orange and basil sauce, and finally a wholemeal fruit crumble with nuts and sunflower seeds.

Well, wonderful, of course. Wonderful. Splendid. Brilliant.

The foods Mrs Foley cooks in Packie's, with their unswerving accent on simple flavours, seem almost a revelation, their taste is so real, so true.

Scallops with Noilly Prat and mushrooms. Confit of duck. Baked turbot with a seed mustard sabayon. Even time-abused classics like Sole meuniere, or crab claws in garlic butter, have stupendous, fresh, vigorous tastes, and that is before you get around to some spoonsome vanilla ice-cream which will beggar belief it is so fine.

You name it, and you will scarcely be able to remember when you last ate it so good. How can someone make gratin of cod with a cheese sauce taste so fine? Produce a breast of chicken in coriander and lime and make it so fresh and appealing? Turn a simple thing like wild smoked salmon with a red onion salsa into something special? Cook a rack of lamb with a redcurrant and mint sauce and make it so sweet? Make a bread and butter pudding with rum so sublime? How does she do it?

Well, wisdom, patience, intuition, and the eternal eagerness of the student, explain Mrs Foley's brilliant work. She never stops learning, never stops experimenting, never stops trying to get better. She has a vision of the perfect restaurant in her mind, and she chases after it each and every day. She doesn't believe she has created it yet. But, some nights, as you enjoy the bliss of her cooking, you know that she has.

■ OPEN:
5.30pm-11pm Mon-Sat (closed Nov-Easter)

■ AVERAGE PRICE:
Dinner from £15. House Wine from £10

■ CREDIT CARDS:
Visa, Access/Master

■ NOTES:
Wine Licence
Wheelchair Access, but not to toilets
Children – welcome, high chair
In the centre of Kenmare.

PARK HOTEL

Francis Brennan
Kenmare, Co Kerry
Tel: (064) 41200 Fax: 41402
e-mail: phkenmre@iol.ie

Head Chef: Bruno Schmidt

If one were to hold a poll of hoteliers, in order to find the hoteliers' hotelier, no one would lay a bet with you that the winner would not be Francis Brennan.

Mr Brennan is, quite simply, the very personification, the very essence, of the hotelier.

His skills are so effortless and so graceful that you can't imagine that he ever actually learnt them, that he ever had to apply himself to understanding the business of entertaining people.

Far more likely, you reckon, that he was born this way, and popped from the womb with this integral and instinctive grasp of how to run an hotel to the very highest standards, and then some.

It is Francis Brennan who personifies and motivates The Park Hotel, articulates its thoughtfulness and appositeness, ensures that the food is correct, that the rooms are perfect, makes it the place it is. He is the man who makes it, in fact, a place like no other place.

And his work also secures the motivation of his team, for when one thinks of dinner in The Park, one thinks of the entire team effort which choreographs this magnificent venture, this lovely room. It is impossible to divorce this fact from the enjoyment of a meal here, for the synchronicity and the service are just as important as the cooking.

One will admire Bruno Schmidt's work in the kitchen for the harmony and well-tuned balance which he brings to his work, and the pure flavours he will produce with a cassoulet of squab with roasted pearl onions, for example, or fillet of codling on angel hair pasta, or veal with a potato galette, or a rabbit cassoulet with a coriander scented emulsion, or perfect grilled wild salmon with crushed new potatoes. The cooking is rich, but well-controlled, the flavours as gracefully orchestrated on the plate as the timing of the staff who serve it.

But the fine food, the superb service with its magical mix of confidence and friendliness, the great wines – especially the clutch of American wines, many of which can only be found in The Park – is just one part of this brilliant tapestry of pleasure, a tapestry without a single trace of preciousness or snobbery.

A final word, perhaps, regarding the work of Jim McCarthy, the head waiter: perfection.

■ OPEN:
7pm-8.45pm Mon-Sun

■ AVERAGE PRICE:
Dinner from £29-£39
House Wine from £16.50

■ CREDIT CARDS:
Visa, Access/Master, Amex, Diners

■ NOTES:
Bar Lunch served, £5-£12
Full Pub Licence
Wheelchair Access
Children – over 6yrs welcome at dinner, menu £5 depending on age and appetite
At the top of the hill in Kenmare town centre.

SHEEN FALLS

Peter MacCann
La Cascade Restaurant
Sheen Falls Lodge
Kenmare, Co Kerry
Tel: (064) 41600 Fax: 41386
e-mail: sheenfalls@iol.ie

Head Chef: Fergus Moore

Fergus Moore has been in charge of the kitchen at Sheen Falls Lodge since the early days of the hotel, and it is his style of luxurious, polite, and well-balanced cooking which has gifted the hotel with its reputation.

Mr Moore's cooking is ambitious in design and execution, but this does not mean that he is a slavish adherent of cuisine Française, or that he merely churns out the latest chic ingredients being used in San Francisco or Sydney.

He likes to use modern French tricks, it is true, for example by shaking up succulent foie gras by means of the vogueish use of balsamic vinegar, and he will play around with classic ideas, so you might find an alliance of smoked duck breast with deep fried haricots.

And he does like to bring in some vogueish ideas from the 'States, serving local oysters with soy marinated leek in a tomato wateressence, for example, or matching loin of venison with a liquorice essence.

But, over the years, he has focused ever more closely on collecting these backgrounds and foregrounds of influence to create a Sheen Falls style, and his discipline means that he produces cooking which is effortlessly enjoyable.

The catholicity of choices on the menu – there are usually half-a-dozen starters and half-a-dozen main courses to choose from, along with salads and a soup, and five desserts – allows one to make up an interesting dinner: air-dried beef with capers, tomato and tarragon is intersected with asparagus spears, and that note of tarragon appears again in a fine chicken consommé with mushrooms. There are classics such as sugar-cured salmon with sweet mustard, and funky things like warm goat's cheese with fried polenta and pesto.

The flavours in a rare tuna steak with a ginger and citrus dressing are refreshingly volatile, and it is perhaps a good idea to go for some of the more modish dishes, for they allow Mr Moore to slip off the flavour restraint that can make some dishes just a little too polite.

The staff in the hotel are quite brilliant, and the wine selection superb, though pricey.

■ OPEN:
7.15pm-9.30pm Mon-Sun

■ AVERAGE PRICE:
Dinner from £37.50
House Wine from £17.50

■ CREDIT CARDS:
Visa, Access/Master, Amex, Diners

■ NOTES:
Breakfast served to non residents, 7.30am-10am Mon-Sun
Full Pub Licence
Full Wheelchair Access
Children – welcome, high chair, special menu
From Kenmare, take the first turn left after the suspension bridge on the road to Glengarriff. Hotel is 1 mile further along.

THE STRAWBERRY TREE

Evan Doyle
24 Plunkett Street
Killarney, Co Kerry
Tel: (064) 32688 Fax: 32688

Head Chef: Eileen O'Brien

Picture this.

You are happily ensconced in the upstairs dining rooms of The Strawberry Tree restaurant, above Yer Man's Pub, in the pulsing, touristic town of Killarney.

You have begun dinner with a parcel of corned beef and cabbage, then moved on to some splendid Kerry mountain lamb with an Irish stew sauce. There may, then, be some bread and butter pudding to finish. As there is a pub downstairs, you may very well drink a pint of stout with dinner.

It all sounds fake, doesn't it? Unreal. Stage Oirish. Tourist cooking for tourists in a tourist town. The waiters probably dress as leprechauns, whilst a coleen plays the harp in the corner of the room.

But it's not fake, it's not ersatz. It is real cooking, real ingredients, using real skill and application and intelligence.

It is real because it is The Strawberry Tree, because Evan Doyle, the owner, is a smart bloke, and because he employs real talent in his kitchens. Mr Doyle doesn't like fake things. He likes real things, and in his career he has shown that he sticks to doing real things with style and wit.

The "Irish" cooking in The Strawberry Tree, then, is real food. Sure, the titles are old – there is boxty, the grated potato pancake; old style fish cakes; Kerry beef accompanied by a traditional brisket; an Irish fish stew; maize cake; rhubarb pudding – but what distinguishes the 'Tree is the care which has gone into sourcing these foods and then cooking them. It may read like traditional Irish cooking, but in fact the application here is as modern as you can get.

Mr Doyle hit on the idea some years ago of sourcing all his foods from local suppliers of unimpeachable quality, so he starts with a major advantage. Pristine local foods – Dennis Barry's duck; Dingle Bay sole; Kerry beef and lamb; wild foods such as nettles and seaweed – are then cooked with imagination and verve. When he started with this idea, Evan Doyle moved himself far ahead of the field, and he remains ahead of them in terms of imagination and accomplishment. The Strawberry Tree is a real restaurant, a place where people try their hardest and do their best.

Thank the heavens that you find it in Killarney.

■ **OPEN:**
6.30pm-10pm Mon-Sat

■ **AVERAGE PRICE:**
Dinner from £24
House Wine from £13.75

■ **CREDIT CARDS:**
Visa, Access/Master, Amex, Diners

■ **NOTES:**
Full Pub Licence
No Wheelchair Access
Children – welcome if well behaved
Centre of Killarney, 50 yards down the street from Glebe Car Park. Stone fronted building on the left hand side.

TONLEGEE HOUSE AND RESTAURANT

Mark & Marjorie Molloy
Athy, Co Kildare
Tel: (0507) 31473 Fax: 31473

Head Chef: Mark Molloy

They have carved out a nice niche for themselves, Mark and Marjorie.

Tonlegee is now a well-established restaurant with rooms, attracting all the smart local folk, and drawing in tourists and visitors during the season.

They come because the Molloys not only have talent, but also have an individual style which is memorable.

Marjorie Molloy, for example, is one of the best front-of-house people in the business. Calm, collected, efficient, welcoming, she is the perfect public face for Mark Molloy's reticent nature.

Mr Molloy prefers to let his food do the talking. He has little public profile, preferring to work away doing what he does, getting it just right. His shyness, and the fact that Tonlegee is a fair hack away from the capital, has perhaps robbed his cooking of some of the acclaim it deserves.

Much appreciated locally, it deserves to be better known, for his work has a novel way with flavours.

For example, he will combine a green bean salad with smoked chicken and croutons, and will make a blue cheese dressing to make the flavours more arresting. This fondness for a counterpointing flavour means that he serves pan fried loin of veal with spinach and a Roquefort sauce. He uses the tense flavour of saffron to add effect to the tomato sauce he prepares for his splendid filo parcel of fresh crabmeat. At every turn, Mr Molloy is trying to offer a fresh perspective on conventional dishes.

But, if he neglected the conservatism of the local market, he wouldn't have a flourishing business, so there are also great crowd pleasers to be enjoyed: stuffed quail on a potato galette; baked goat's cheese with tomato and tapenade; celery soup with toasted hazelnuts; fillet of beef with a mustard and tarragon sauce; noisettes of lamb en croute with ratatouille; pear tarte tatin with vanilla ice cream; chocolate truffle cake with a coffee bean sauce.

The significant fact about Tonlegee is the precision with which Mark Molloy cooks, and the charm with which Marjorie Molloy takes care of the restaurant. They are one of the great double acts in the business, producing smashing food in a lovely house.

■ **OPEN:**
7pm-9pm Mon-Thur, 7pm-10.30pm Fri-Sat
■ **AVERAGE PRICE:**
Dinner from £22
House Wine £9.50
■ **CREDIT CARDS:**
Visa, Access/Master, Amex

■ **NOTES:**
Restaurant Licence
No Wheelchair Access
Children – welcome if well behaved
In Athy, cross two bridges and take the Kilkenny road out of town. Very soon you will see their sign telling you to go left.

CAFÉ SOL

Eavan Kenny & Gail Johnson
William Street, Kilkenny
Co Kilkenny
Tel: (056) 64987

Head Chef: Gail Johnson

Eavan Kenny and Gail Johnson carved out an enviable reputation when they cooked a few miles south of the city, in Bennettsbridge, and when they decamped into the big smoke of Kilkenny, they brought with them their sassy, smart cooking and their winning style of running a restaurant.

Quite simply, these girls know how to make a room work. They know how to create a space where you want to sit right down and chill right out. They put together the mix of breezy atmosphere, quality consciousness and good value as perfectly and as subtly as a good bartender making a Bloody Mary. And when they mix it, you want to drink it. And have another.

Café Sol is a simple, square room, perfectly delightful at lunchtime when it is thronged with locals who adore this flavourful, good value cooking. The lunch menu is eclectic but well-chosen, a moreish mix of sandwiches, vegetarian dishes such as nachos with chilli sauce, cheese and salad; salads such as chicken livers with green lentils, and splendid main dishes such as the lovely Lavistown sausages – made just outside the city by Olivia Goodwillie – with cracking mash and a fine mustard mayonnaise.

This is the food the girls like: fun to make, fun to eat, easy on the tastebuds and the pocket.

In the evening, the blinds are drawn and the candles lit, and the menu opens out: breast of duck with honey, apple and rosemary; chicken with mozzarella and Parma ham; pasta with tomato, chilli and basil; good scallops and steaks with red wine sauce. Nothing gets in the way of the flavours of the food, and this unpretentious cooking is designed to please, to satisfy, and it achieves this effortlessly.

This honesty perhaps reveals the influence of the time the girls spent with Myrtle Allen in Ballymaloe House, but, unlike other some graduates of that institution, they have moved their cooking onwards, changing it along the way into a lighter, more unpredictable, and rather more modish concoction, which wears their signature proudly. It's fun food, and the Kilkenny bourgeoisie, and the Kilkenny tourists, and the Kilkenny festival set, all love it to bits.

And, of course, you will too.

■ **OPEN:**
10am-6pm Mon-Sat, noon-4pm Sun, 7pm-10pm Wed-Sat

■ **AVERAGE PRICE:**
Lunch £5.50. Dinner from £20
House Wine from £9.50

■ **CREDIT CARDS:**
Visa, Access/Master

■ **NOTES:**
Wine Licence
Wheelchair Access
Children – welcome if well behaved
At Kilkenny castle, go through traffic lights onto High Street, second turn left, William Street, restaurant opposite Town Hall.

LACKEN HOUSE ✪

Eugene & Breda McSweeney
Dublin Road, Kilkenny
Co Kilkenny
Tel: (056) 61085 Fax: 62435
e-mail: lackenhs@indigo.ie

Head Chef: Eugene McSweeney

Invention and tradition. Regionalism and internationalism. The personal and the professional.

That diplomat of good food, Eugene McSweeney, brings all these ingredients together in his cooking in Lacken House, fuses these competing pressures perfectly into a cuisine which is proud and proudly delicious.

You could select any dish from the menus which Mr McSweeney prepares and cooks in Lacken House, a homely, peaceful restaurant with rooms which he and his wife Breda run just on the outskirts of Kilkenny, and no matter what the choice, and no matter what the individual tastes and the distinct techniques which will be involved, you will find yourself always confronted by two simple truths.

The first is that with everything he cooks, Mr McSweeney exploits the long-learnt skill of the professional cook. Skill, here, is used to extract flavour, to reveal the character and essence of a food. Starters such as house marinated salmon with a hot colcannon potato cake and a dill and mustard sauce, or the wonderful crab gateau, or a venison sausage with a garlic mash, will taste as good as they can possibly taste. They will taste, quite simply, of themselves. That is what good cooking is.

Secondly, you will also find that the cooking shows someone who has never lost touch with the scents, attractions and satisfactions of the garden and the ground: a splendid nettle pesto served with a simple vegetable soup; dynamic essence of mushroom broth; pigeon wrapped in bacon with a barley risotto; wild boar with candied pears and a cream game sauce; loin of lamb with a tansy mousse. Extraordinary flavours, some of them likely to be amongst the very best you have tasted.

If he is a good cook, he is also a wise cook, keeping his chain of suppliers as short as possible, with almost everything culled from local suppliers.

And local, also, is the character of Lacken House, the staff are warmly welcoming, and you find the true tastes of Irish food, and Irish hospitality, here. Breda McSweeney is one of the finest sommeliers in the country, and her expertise is the perfect addendum to her husband's inventiveness and perfectionism.

■ OPEN:
7pm-10.30pm Tue-Sat
■ AVERAGE PRICE:
Dinner from £22
House Wine from £12
■ CREDIT CARDS:
Visa, Access/Master, Amex, Diners

■ NOTES:
Restaurant Licence
No Wheelchair Access
Children – welcome, high chair, special menu
On the Dublin Road, just as you drive into Kilkenny from Carlow, just past the roundabout on the right hand side.

THE MOTTE

Alan Walton & Tom Reade-Duncan
Inistioge
Co Kilkenny
Tel: (056) 58655

Head Chef: Alan Walton

There is a great sense of playfulness and enjoyment about the food, the cooking and the atmosphere in The Motte, and they really do like to have fun with their cooking, do Alan and Tom. Expect the unexpected when you walk into The Motte. Like this:

White gazpacho with smoked salmon. Garlic fried prawn and sun-dried tomato kebab. Toulouse sausage with a pickled cabbage salad. Breast of chicken with peach and chilli.

Slightly strange combinations – think of that sausage with a pickled cabbage salad, how unorthodox! – slightly unexpected, but well achieved, carefully considered, when you come to consider it. And fun. Yes, fun.

They have always enjoyed this playfulness with ingredients, right back in the days when the Motte was situated in the centre of Inistioge, before it moved to its brand new, rather discreet and unassuming home, just a few hundred yards outside the most filmed and photographed village in the country.

In the early days, when the restaurant was back in the village, when you might be served pork fillet cooked in coconut milk, or roast pheasant with a chocolate sauce, they were busy having fun with food, adding twists and turns that caused you to light up with pleasure. Clever, fun food, and very well controlled.

But, of course, they are prudent restaurateurs, not just showmen, and so alongside their inventions and improvisations, there is a rock solid selection of ever-popular dishes.

Horseradish crusted roast cod with garlic and pepper sauce.

Sirloin steak with an onion marmalade.

Stuffed guinea fowl with a sherry and redcurrant sauce.

Barbary duck with a pear and red onion sauce.

Good things, enjoyable things, but even the conventional here has little variations, little grace notes. But, even if you shy clear of the more outlandish and inventive dishes on the menu, and play it somewhat safe, the central rule of The Motte is ever-present: this is a fun place, somewhere to have a good time. Alan and Tom work hard to make sure that happens, making sure value for money is excellent, and that service and ambience are just right.

■ **OPEN:**
7pm-9.30pm Tue-Sat
■ **AVERAGE PRICE:**
Dinner from £21
House Wine from £10.75
■ **CREDIT CARDS:**
Visa, Access/Master

■ **NOTES:**
Wine Licence
No Wheelchair Access (but happy to help)
Children – over 12 yrs only
500m from the Square in Inistioge, on the Thomastown/Kilkenny road.

THE WATERSIDE

Daniel & Catherine Fitzpatrick
The Quay
Graiguenamanagh
Co Kilkenny
Tel: (0503) 24246 Fax: 24733

Head Chef: Daniel Fitzpatrick

Daniel Fitzpatrick is a good cook. He can take the dishes which others march quickly into routine – a warm goat's cheese salad is one that comes to mind, something more complex such as a terrine of duck is another – and he can make them as lively and fresh tasting and as enjoyable to eat as if he was making them for the very first time.

This is the indicator of his professionalism, and it is assisted by his innovative touches in the kitchen.

In a world of recipes which involve Clonakilty black pudding, he likes to serve the pud in brioche, with a port sauce and sautéed apples, and will team his smoked salmon with a lemon dill cream.

Throughout his menus in The Waterside, a fine old mill building which the Fitzpatricks have transformed into a restaurant with accommodation, there are the signs of a serious, accomplished cook.

If he makes a fine duck terrine, he can also cook the breast of duck as well as a Frenchman, the slices of juicy meat in a rich port sauce. And he likes to play off the sweet taste of turbot with some endive and an anchovy butter fumé, an alliance he will also make with grilled sea bass.

Alongside these clever touches, there are classics such as mussels steamed with white wine and shallots, Jim Delaney's fillet steak with a peppercorn sauce, loin of Callan pork with caramelised apples, tagliatelle with tomato sauce and basil, and a thoughtful vegetarian hot pot with truffle oil. Everything is distinguished by a steady professionalism and confidence, right down to excellent desserts such as iles flottante, home-made ice creams and crème brûlée.

At lunchtime during summer there is a more informal menu: soups, salads, sandwiches and main courses such as Toulouse sausage with mash and mustard, or breast of chicken with mushroom sauce. The wine list is most impressive, and boasts a fine selection of both organic and biodynamic wines.

The ability to stay overnight is a major attraction of The Waterside, and the rooms are thoughtful and comfy. If you are taking a pre-dinner stroll in Graigue, be sure to check out M. Doyle's splendid bar and shop, on the Main Street, a little piece of the past perfectly preserved and presented.

■ **OPEN:**
12.30pm-2.30pm, 7pm-10pm Mon-Sun (off season dinner only Wed-Sat & Sun lunch)
■ **AVERAGE PRICE:**
Lunch £10.95. Dinner from £18
House Wine from £11.25
■ **CREDIT CARDS:**
Visa, Access/Master

■ **NOTES:**
Restaurant Licence
Wheelchair Access, but not to toilets
Children – welcome 'till 8pm, high chair, special menu, £6.50
On the river front.

PRESTON HOUSE

Allison Dowling
Abbeyleix, Co Laois
Tel: (0502) 31432 Fax: 31432

Head Chef: Allison Dowling

Preston House Café is a noble stone building in the centre of Abbeyleix village, converted by Allison and Michael Dowling from an old Protestant boy's school, into a restaurant with rooms.

And it is here that Allison Dowling prepares food which does nothing less than make you feel good.

Mrs Dowling's cooking has always had this gift. For some years she ran a sparkling little country house a few miles south of Abbeyleix. Glebe House was a delightful place, a little hideaway where you could forget the rest of the world and immerse yourself in the sort of cooking that gave you an appetite the instant you saw it.

People fell in love with the place, with the food and the comfort, above all with Allison Dowling's affable and calming manner.

The food in Preston House is simple country cooking, and it can be perfect. Braised beef with vegetables, a gentle braise of meat and root vegetables, served with perfectly cooked cabbage and some boiled potatoes. Chicken fillets in a white wine sauce with rice, light, well-judged. Pan fried trout with a garden salad, the fish fresh and brisk, the leaves crisp and invigorating. Warm salad with Rudd's ham, the local Abbey Blue brie, walnuts and croûtons, a perfect play of good ingredients.

Desserts are true nursery time treats: apple and blackberry crumble, banana splits, peaches in Bushmills.

And Mrs Dowling's generous manner is an integral part of her cooking. She cooks the food she likes to eat and the food she reckons people will enjoy best of all, that sort of simple comfort food which, in Mrs Dowling's hands, screams out, Try Me!

So, at dinnertime there might be tomato and basil soup, then some roast leg of lamb with redcurrant jelly, or perhaps chicken with almonds and wholegrain mustard, these served with green runner beans and courgettes, then lemon ice cream or fruit charlotte pudding.

One evening, we had a dinner of smoked haddock chowder, and then a sirloin with mushrooms in cream, new potatoes and carrots. There was a fine salad, then an excellent crème brûlée. It was the sort of food that could scarcely be better, the sort of food that is good for body and soul. Feel good food, from a cook who sees this as her highest ambition, and knows how to achieve it.

■ **OPEN:**
10am-9pm Thur-Sat, 10.30am-5.30pm Sun
■ **AVERAGE PRICE:**
Sunday Lunch £12 (mid week à la carte)
Dinner £20
House Wine from £10
■ **CREDIT CARDS:**
Visa, Access/Master

■ **NOTES:**
Wine Licence
Wheelchair Access
Children – welcome, high chair
On the main street in Abbeyleix.

THE MUSTARD SEED AT ECHO LODGE

Daniel Mullane
Ballingarry, Co Limerick
Tel: (069) 68508 Fax: 68511

Head Chef: David Norris

"The house feels like it has been here for ever", Dan Mullane says of Echo Lodge, and it most certainly does.

But Dan Mullane has only been here for a few years, so his achievement in creating a space with such a timeless feel is mighty impressive. That he has succeeded will come as no surprise to those who knew his work in The Mustard Seed, when it was housed in a dreamily nostalgic thatched cottage in Adare village, seven miles back up the road in the direction of Limerick.

The Mustard Seed was one of the most successful, and enjoyable, restaurants in Ireland, and its success and its enjoyability were founded on a simple pretext. Mr Mullane made it a place where everything was right, and felt right, a place where everything worked. It was a restaurant which trumpeted all of the good bits that make restaurants special, memorable, places, and which seemed to have managed to ditch all the bad bits which make restaurants exasperating. Dan Mullane has pulled off this coup once again, in Echo Lodge.

The use of colour, for example, works here because at times its use is restrained, and then suddenly the bright shock from the Villeroy and Bosch plates will leap out at you. There are few paintings throughout the house, but the use of photographs, prints, and covers from magazines such as American "Gourmet", works perfectly – slightly ironic, and yet effective.

David Norris is the chef, and his style continues the "Modern Irish Cooking" which was achieved so successfully at The Mustard Seed. Principal ingredients meet with friendly partners: grilled goat's cheese on a waldorf salad with a beetroot and chive dressing; wood pigeon on braised lentils with matchstick potatoes and a port gravy; spring lamb on a lightly curried pasta – a novel touch – with a coriander and apricot jus.

And, of course, there are classics such as beef with a peppercorn crust and a port and thyme jus, or grilled turbot on a wild garlic, lemon and mustard beurre blanc, orange pudding with a vanilla anglaise, homemade ice creams with a warm butterscotch sauce. Like the house, the food mixes classicism with modernism, but keeps a clear focus on the ambition to do things right which drives Mr Mullane.

■ OPEN:
7pm-9.30pm Mon-Sun
Closed Sun & Mon off season

■ AVERAGE PRICE:
Dinner from £28-£30
House Wine from £12.95

■ CREDIT CARDS:
Visa, Access/Master, Amex

■ NOTES:
Restaurant Licence
Full Wheelchair Access
Children – welcome, high chair
Killarney road from Adare for 1/4 mile.
Take the first left (R519) to Ballingarry.

QUENELLES RESTAURANT

Kieran & Sindy Pollard
Upper Henry Street, Limerick
Co Limerick
Tel: (061) 411111 Fax: 400111

Head Chef: Kieran Pollard

Limerick used to get the most terrible press of any city in Ireland.

"Best seen through a rear-view mirror" was the kiss-off summation of one writer a few years back, a remark which stung the locals.

Well, they must have decided to do something about it, for Limerick now feels like a city on the move, a place breezy with optimism and progress, and restaurateurs like Kieran and Sindy Pollard are vital players in this regeneration.

For if Limerick used to be a dull place to visit, it used to be a deadly place to eat, its restaurants managing to combine a thunderous pretentiousness with dodgy cooking. We were once served some fresh foie gras in a restaurant here, and for a garnish the chef decorated the plate with shredded iceberg lettuce. That's the kind of thing you used to get in Limerick.

Not any more. Mr Pollard and his wife have carved out a space in Quenelle's which is both chic and cosmopolitan. We know that those are two words one would never have associated with Limerick in the past, but Mr Pollard has brought a wealth of experience and suss back from his travels and his time in Australia, and he puts it to work in Quenelles.

These Asiatic influences can be seen in the way in which he will scent a bowl of duck broth with coriander, and team butternut squash with coconut. He likes to work his twist on local foods also: a doughnut of Meg Gordon's Inagh goat's cheese will come with sweet butter onions and pine nuts, and a zested winter cabbage and a marmalade beurre blanc, a terrific success.

This is Mr Pollard's strength: he can mix and match tastes and textures to come up with something new and enticing, however wild the mixes can sometimes seem, and in the intimate charm of the restaurant it works a treat: cutlets of Irish lamb with a roast and apricot stuffed quail; a smoked apple and honey Dijon mustard sauce with a roast loin of pork; sirloin of Irish beef with a layer of yams and a bell pepper sauce; crab and winter vegetable puddings with a roast almond and carrot glaze; garden vegetables with blackened bananas in a sour yogurt and avocado dough. Desserts are as imaginative as the savoury cooking.

The wine list is good, service is excellent, and this is the restaurant Limerick has been waiting a long time for. Keep an eye on Mr Pollard.

■ **OPEN:**
7pm-9.15pm Tue-Sat
■ **AVERAGE PRICE:**
Dinner from £24
House Wine from £10.95
■ **CREDIT CARDS:**
Visa, Access/Master, Amex

■ **NOTES:**
Restaurant Licence
No Wheelchair Access
Children – over 8yrs welcome
On the corner between Henry Street and Mallow Street in the centre of town.

THE WILD GEESE

Con Roche & Serge Coustrain
Rose Cottage,
Adare, Co Limerick
Tel: (061) 396451 Fax: 396451

Head Chef: Serge Coustrain

They are a good twosome, Mr Roche and M. Coustrain, a front-of-house man and a cook who brought a considerable depth of experience with them to the lovely space which is the Wild Geese, the restaurant formerly owned by Dan Mullane and known as The Mustard Seed.

Mr Roche is a Dubliner, M. Coustrain from Toulon, and they shared spells working together in both Dromoland Castle and the Castletroy Park Hotel, before deciding to set up shop together and moving down the road from Limerick to Adare.

Right from the outset, and no doubt conscious that they were taking over a restaurant which was not merely many people's favourite, but which had also won world-wide renown, they stated their ambitions: "Every guest is important to us and we will do our utmost to ensure that your meal with us is a memorable one", they wrote, a statement which should be the intent of every restaurant in the country.

Well, the premises certainly helps to make a meal memorable. The Wild Geese is set in a thatched cottage in the loveliest village in Ireland, its interior a calming series of connecting rooms.

Here, M. Coustrain offers a broad menu which changes with the seasons – he particularly enjoys game cookery when the season is on, and offers special menus at this time of year.

Otherwise, his style is to offer a selection of classics and variations thereon: steamed asparagus with hollandaise; Inagh goat's cheese with rocket and beetroot salad; queen scallops served on the shell with garlic breadcrumbs; squab with pan-fried foie gras.

But if his background is classical, M. Coustrain does like to cut loose with his main courses: with a peppered duck breast he will add some smoked garlic; with rack of lamb and field mushrooms he will serve some deep-fried goat's cheese dumplings; he will send out fillets of brill with basmati rice and coconut milk sauce; he may stuff a savoy cabbage with confit of duck, or breadcrumb an escalope of salmon and then deep fry it, and match it with a beansprout roll.

This is pleasing cooking, from a chef who works hard. Indeed, this is a team who work hard together, to make a meal a memorable event.

■ OPEN:
11am-5pm Tue-Sat, 6.30pm-10pm Tue-Sat
■ AVERAGE PRICE:
Dinner £27
House Wine from £12.50
■ CREDIT CARDS:
Visa, Access/Master, Amex, Diners

■ NOTES:
Full Pub Licence
Wheelchair Access, but not to toilets
Children – over 10yrs welcome
Directly opposite the Dunraven Arms Hotel at the top of the village (Limerick side).

JORDAN'S TOWNHOUSE & RESTAURANT

Harry & Marian Jordan
Newry Street, Carlingford
Co Louth
Tel: (042) 73223 Fax: 73827

Head Chefs: Harry & Marian Jordan

Harry and Marian Jordan call their style of cooking "parochial", but don't imagine this means something cautious and dated, something parish-pumpish.

Don't be fooled by such a modest term, because "parochial", in Jordan's, means cooking which reflects the strength of the parish.

And the parish can offer fine local oysters from Carlingford Bay, and fine field mushrooms collected nearby. There will be local fish, and good herbaceous meats. The Jordans themselves describe it as "simply a style that attempts to inspire local pride, and respect, for all the good produce that surrounds us". Their skills mean that this proud mantra, an invocation to regional cooking which should be trumpeted from every corner of the country, is brought vividly to life on the plate.

A weekend dinner, then, might produce excellent crab claws with garlic butter and a fish stock vinaigrette, or perhaps a thumpingly fine array of oysters which come, two-by-two, with warmed pesto, with some chunky provençale sauce, and resplendently plain.

Then a truly marvellous bowl of curried parsnip soup – a definition of the soupmaker's art, and an aleph of what Harry and Marian's style is all about: simple, soulful, satisfying, the same sort of ambitions found in main courses such as a meltingly tender shank of mountain lamb – their signature dish, and deservedly so – or perhaps an excellent darne of cod, which had been marinated in gremolata and then oven baked. It is simple cooking, but it is so well understood, and so intuitively appreciative of the rich flavours enjoyed by the food itself, that it is delightful.

Although they have been hard at work for a dozen years now, the Jordans have an energy and raucousness in their work which is inspiring.

Partly this may be explained by the fact that they alternate in the kitchen: Harry cooks one night, Marian the next, and they alternate cooking with working the front of house, a method which not only staves off fatigue, but also likely inspires some keen competition between the couple.

But their success is also explained by the fact that they are proud of their place and their village, proud of their parish. "Parochial" never tasted so good.

■ OPEN:
6.30pm-9.45pm Mon-Sat
12.30pm-2.30pm Sun

■ AVERAGE PRICE:
Sunday Lunch £13. Dinner £22.50
House Wine from £9.95

■ CREDIT CARDS:
Visa, Access/Master, Amex

■ NOTES:
Full Pub Licence
No Wheelchair Access
Children – welcome, high chair
Centre of Carlingford.

ECHOES

Siobhan, Tom & Helen Ryan
Main Street, Cong, Co Mayo
Tel: (092) 46059 Fax 46665

Head Chef: Siobhan Ryan

Siobhan Ryan is a good cook, with a style that happily embraces a culinary vocabulary of lusty, trusty, friendly tastes.

Eating her food, one is struck by the fact that she very obviously loves to cook. There is a freshness of approach, a timelessness, and a well-defined logic and simplicity, to her work.

Like the best women chefs, she is determined first and foremost to produce food which is enjoyable to eat and which has all the appropriate flavours intact, and her menus aim to offer something for most everyone, from simple Irish stew to fresh lobster, from smoked salmon on a simple bed of salad, to black sole fried and served with lemon.

She likes, for example, to roast a rack of lamb and serve it with a grilled aubergine and rosemary sauce.

Blissful, admirable, though truth be told the irrepressible flavour of the lamb will almost scarcely need the solid, comforting and zappy sauce, for the quality of meat found in Echoes is superlative, so good that you just want to pick it up and eat it with your fingers.

If you enquire as to just how they manage to effect this narcotic of meaty flavour, aside from Ms Ryan's skill, they will tell you that the meat is especially fine because Siobhan's dad, Tom, runs the butcher's shop, just next door to the restaurant.

There is nothing quite like having unimpeachable supply sources right on your doorstep, but Ms Ryan reaches farther out, and her ability to source fine local fish and shellfish – she pan fries scallops with either cheese and paprika, or garlic and smoked bacon, and whips up a lime hollandaise for salmon – completes the axis around which her flavoursome, friendly food revolves.

This is very personal, uncomplicated, logical and unpretentious cooking, and at times – particularly those times when you have maybe had a long day touring Mayo, or a long day with the fish eluding you, it is exactly what you want.

Desserts are big, lush, lascivious affairs, with the brown bread ice cream something of a legend, both locally and internationally.

This deeply comforting food, full of odoriferous scents and rich with goodness, comes in grandly generous portions, and the happy family affair of Echoes is a haven of simplicity, decency and delight

■ OPEN:
5pm-10pm Mon-Sun (7pm-10pm Thur-Sun during winter season)

■ AVERAGE PRICE:
Dinner from £15-£20
House Wine from £11

■ CREDIT CARDS:
Visa, Access/Master, Amex

■ NOTES:
Full Pub Licence
No Wheelchair Access
Children – welcome, high chair
Right in the centre of Cong. Look out for the lilac/purple building on the main street of the village.

CROMLEACH LODGE

Christy & Moira Tighe
Castlebaldwin, Boyle
Co Sligo
Tel: (071) 65155 Fax: 65455
cromleac@iol.ie

Head Chef: Moira Tighe

Moira Tighe has progressed steadily, collectedly, interestingly, as a chef in the last five years.

Back then, she tended to wear her influences a little too much on the sleeve of her whites, a fact which shielded her own accomplishments under the shadow of other cooks.

But, as time has gone on and Cromleach has matured and progressed, Mrs Tighe has found her style, and eating in Cromleach introduces one to a cook with a lively, original and fun way of doing things.

She will take a confit of duck, for example, and flake it and use it to dress a crispy potato galette. She makes an excellent tartlet of quail breasts and pairs them wisely with the chunky flavour of creamed noodles. Her sausage of chicken mousse on a carrot and Sauternes sauce is now a modern classic, and cannot be taken off the menu. It is a great invention: light, flavourful, a perfect starter.

And she likes to have fun with simple things like soups and salads, creating a lively, fun salad with a collation of pristine leaves and toasted pine nuts, and serving a trio of spot-on soups in tiny coffee cups. Nice work, witty and absorbing both for the eye and the palate.

This sort of work shows a cook who is having fun with the games and schemes of presentation, and it is a confident touch which continues with the main courses.

A garlic and herb crust will be wrapped around noisettes of Sligo lamb; she will pair veal and venison together with a simple mustard and port sauce; wild salmon comes with excellent creamed spring onions.

Desserts have always been a speciality of Cromleach, and they are productions worthy of Busby Berkeley: fabulous iced pineapple soufflé, a marvellous tiramisu scented with Tia Maria, splendid banana and chocolate mousse. You can pay a little extra for a tasting plate of desserts, and it is worth the money.

It is a pity that the dining rooms in Cromleach are split up and on different levels, for it would be more fun to see a big happy room of people enjoying this smart cooking all together. The formality of the service is impressive, but perhaps a little more informality might suit the zeitgeist, the creative spirit, of Cromleach Lodge a little better.

■ OPEN:
7pm-9pm Mon-Sat, 6.30pm-8pm Sun
■ AVERAGE PRICE:
Dinner from £25-£35
House Wine from £12.95
■ CREDIT CARDS:
Visa, Access/Master, Amex, Diners

■ NOTES:
Full Pub Licence
Wheelchair Access with assistance
Children – welcome, high chair, half price menu
Signposted from Castlebaldwin on the N4, 8 miles west of Boyle, 17 miles east of Sligo.

GLEBE HOUSE RESTAURANT

Marc & Brid Torrades
Collooney, Co Sligo
Tel: (071) 67787 Fax: 30438

Head Chefs: Brid Torrades
Dominik Bissenger

Brid Torrades and her team cook food that is good for body and soul.

There is something so elemental and earthy about her work – whether it is deep, soulful taste of a bowl of garden vegetable and green herb soup, or the rich sweetness of a confit leg of duck, or the freshness and unadulterated vigour of a salad of garden leaves – that it impresses as food you could eat every day, never mind just every week or every month.

Like the best female cooks, she works in a style which seems unmediated, and she can get her crew to produce food which boasts, firstly, of its own flavours and, then, of the flavours of the area.

So, simple things like gnocchi Parisienne – made with choux pastry – will have their effete, melt-in-the-mouth texture offset by creamed wild mushrooms, making the dish wilder and more robust. The herbs used in her soups can seem to have had their concentrated scents extracted from them, and her cooking of the local beef and lamb – the former perhaps paired with rosemary and green peppercorns, the latter with garlic and thyme – shows a cook who is chasing after the very scents of the earth.

It is comfort cooking, but it is spirited and immensely enjoyable in the simple space that is Glebe House.

Marc and Brid Torrades bought the house when it was little more than a ruin, and have steadily set to putting it to rights over the years, at the same time as having a family and running Glebe as a B&B. During that time they have built an impressive local following, people who appreciate just how much Brid appreciates her work, how much she enjoys and respects the business of food and wine.

The dining rooms are simple, largely unadorned, and perhaps some white tablecloths would be a good idea to brighten them up. The service, by sparky young women like Lucia and Valerie, is pure darling, and Glebe has always been someplace you feel very well looked after.

Mrs Torrades always wears a simple cook's cap when she is about her work, and it is a good indicator of the type of cook she is. Modest, accomplished, professional, a woman who understands and enjoys the scents and satisfactions of the kitchen, she is committed to her work and to her team.

■ **OPEN:**
6.30pm-9.30pm Mon-Sun
Closed Sun & Mon off season
■ **AVERAGE PRICE:**
Dinner from £18.95
House Wine from £9.95
■ **CREDIT CARDS:**
Visa, Access/Master, Amex, Diners

■ **NOTES:**
Wine Licence. Wheelchair Access
Children – welcome, high chair, half price, or according to what is served
7 miles from Sligo city, 1/2 mile from Collooney on the Collooney/Coolaney Rd.

TRUFFLES ✪

Bernadette O'Shea
11 The Mall, Sligo, Co Sligo
Tel:(071) 44226

Head chef: Bernadette O'Shea

If one were to write an ABC of Truffles, a little kiddies book to introduce toddlers to the good food in Bernadette O'Shea's unique restaurant, how might it go?

A, for absolutely amazing.
B, for blissful, brilliant.
C, for cataclysmic.
D, for dazzling, delirious.
E, for euphoric.
F, for fantastic.

And so on, and so on. Ms O'Shea's cooking is a cuisine of superlatives, nothing less. There is no other cook like her, and no one who can do what she does. She is a maverick, a one-off, one of the most skilled and creative talents at work in an Irish kitchen.

She has not only pioneered a totally different cuisine from anyone else in the country, she has also pioneered a totally different way of running a restaurant. Truffles is orchestrated around Ms O'Shea's dynamic creativity. It is both a shrine to her skills, and a laboratory for her experiments. Whilst the cooking here is amongst the finest in the country, you can neither book a table, nor expect a linen table cloth and liveried staff. Bernadette O'Shea's experiment involves running a restaurant where food and enjoyment is the crucial epicentre of the experience. All the other flim-flam of the restaurant game is dispensed with. Total food. Total cooking. Total commitment. Total deliciousness. Total creativity.

The principal constituent of Truffles' cooking is the remarkable pizzas which are the mainstay of the menu. There are classics such as the quattro stagioni, or something simple like pizza with pepperoni. Then there are the modern Irish classics: Milleens cheese with fresh seasonal herbs, enriched with cream cheese, garlic, sun-dried tomatoes and a precise scattering of chives, basil, oregano and thyme. The astounding black pudding and leek pizza with pine nuts, the grains of the pudding glistening like caviar. The stunning cabbage and Parma ham, with a trio of cheeses. No one else can make these. No one else would even think of them. They are amongst the greatest flavours you can enjoy.

But everything in Truffles is perfection. The brilliant salads with local cheeses and roasted red peppers. The foccaccia baked with garlic and fresh tomatoes. The polenta baked with a gorgonzola sauce. The wantonish flavours of the desserts. The great wine list, the great service. 26 letters is just too few superlatives.

■ OPEN:
7pm-9pm Mon-Sat, 6.30pm-8pm Sun
■ AVERAGE PRICE:
Dinner from £25-£35
House Wine from £12.95
■ CREDIT CARDS:
Visa, Access/Master, Amex, Diners

■ NOTES:
Full Pub Licence
Wheelchair Access with assistance
Children – welcome, high chair, half price menu
On the Enniskillen road out of Sligo.

BROCKA-ON-THE-WATER

Anthony & Anne Gernon
Kilgarvan Quay, Ballinderry
Co Tipperary
Tel: (067) 22038

Head Chef: Nancy Byrne

No matter where you might eat in Ireland, there is no one place like Nancy Byrne and Anne Gernon's Brocka-on-the-Water.

The Water is the lovely lakeshore of Lough Derg, in Tipperary, and the restaurant itself is just outside Ballinderry, where you turn off that delightful meandering road which runs between Portumna and Puckane and then on into Nenagh. The restaurant is just like a domestic house, albeit one which has been turned into a restaurant, but the domestic imprimatur is still pre-eminent. Walking into Brocka is like walking into a friend's house for dinner.

If the atmosphere is stylishly domestic, the food drives this message home with vigour. Both Anne and her mum, Nancy, cook, and they bring forth food which has that element of intuition and command you might have imagined had vanished. As a friend remarked, "Brocka is an example of the perfection of domestic cooking".

They use the Tipperary cheese, Cooleeney, to make a delightful croquette, paired with a fine, spicy chutney. They have locally smoked salmon trout and mackerel which they confect into an aptly judged salad with a sundried tomato dressing, and they make a bowl of spinach and garden vegetable soup which is so effervescent with fresh green flavours that it just about takes your breath away.

Ribbons of chicken with root ginger and honey, baked stuffed sole fillet with a chervil and lemon cream, all have the care and consideration of good cooking, whilst beef fillet with fresh horseradish and a black pepper cream is so mellow and moreish and so much a statement of what good, homely cooking is all about that you simply lose yourself in oohs and aahs of pleasure, that relaxed pleasure which comes from true, generous, maternal cooking.

Indeed, this is food which almost makes the critic redundant, for its essence lies not with being admired and judged – with being examined – as with simply enjoying it.

As you nibble some farmhouse cheeses, or lovely desserts of stuffed pears with marzipan and a butterscotch sauce, or homemade chocolate cake or some ice cream with raspberries and kirsch, you realise you are smitten. For what else can you do with this food, but fall in love with it?

■ OPEN:
7pm-10pm Mon-Sat

■ AVERAGE PRICE:
Dinner £24
House Wine from £14

■ CREDIT CARDS:
No Credit Cards

■ NOTES:
Restaurant Licence
No Wheelchair Access
Children – welcome
On Kilgarvan Quay on the Lough Derg Drive, half way between Nenagh and Portumna.

CHEZ HANS

Hans Peter & Jason Matthias
Cashel
Co Tipperary
Tel: (062) 61177
Fax: 61177

Head Chef: Hans Matthias

"Thank you, Lord, for preserving me to eat another dinner at Chez Hans".

So intoned the jowly, prelate-perfect man who had, clearly, strolled out of the pages of G.K. Chesterton, as he laid down his knife and fork.

He spoke for us all.

With the image of the Last Supper staring down at you with its poignant bitterness, the fact that Chez Hans was formerly a church makes it the perfect place to break bread, especially in the company of the prelate-perfect types you can often find in here.

Chez Hans' secret lies in its magical ability, despite twenty-five years of business, to make every evening seem like a first night. The staff are sweet, keen and professional, and only the music leaves anything to be desired: with that vaulting roof and the sun-comprehending glass, you tend to want to hear Bach cantatas.

Jason Matthias has now taken over the kitchen of the restaurant his father founded even before he was a baby, adding a modernism to a restaurant whose food has always been punchy and sustaining.

He likes to cook fish, sourcing lobster from Kinsale, making a gratin of Rossmore oysters, pairing turbot with Dublin Bay prawns, but the fondness for meat – and lots of it – which is an element of country restaurants is not neglected: Tipperary lamb with a herb crust is as elementally flavourful as the local beef, whilst quail with wild mushrooms will be perfectly roasted and will have achieved that glorious, irresistible richness which forces you to eat the birds with your fingers. This is unapologetically sumptuous food.

Vegetables in Chez Hans are, it seems, prepared for someone who is girding themselves to gather winter wheat by hand: mounds of spicy champ, a lather of crisp carrots, lots and lots of broccoli, a drumlin of creamy mushrooms.

Excellent desserts, good coffee and then, like all the happy families and couples and clerics, with their well-fed smiles and their contented relaxation, you will mutter "Thank you, Lord, for preserving me to eat another dinner at Chez Hans". The prelate-perfect man out of the pages of G.K. Chesterton said it. Everyone thinks it.

■ **OPEN:**
6.30pm-9.30pm Tue-Sat

■ **AVERAGE PRICE:**
Dinner £22
House Wine £10.50

■ **CREDIT CARDS:**
Visa, Access/Master

■ **NOTES:**
Restaurant Licence
Wheelchair Access
Children – welcome
Just beside the Rock of Cashel, and clearly signposted from the Dublin-Cork road as you come into Cashel going south.

WATERMAN'S LODGE

Brid Ryan
Ballina
Killaloe
Co Tipperary
Tel: (061) 376333
Fax: 375030

Head Chef: James Hunt

We think the air of content and calm which exudes from Waterman's Lodge, Brid Ryan's restaurant and country house, in Ballina, County Tipperary, can be ascribed to a fairly simple reason.

It is a house where the use of contents, and the style of food, seems to be guided by the defining principle that the Lodge should have all it needs – and absolutely no more.

So it enjoys the appropriate sofas, the appropriate flowers, the appropriate cooking, and yet in the era of downsizing, in the times of chic simple in which we live, here is a house whose essential simplicity and modesty does the heart good. In short, it is a place where things are deeply, carefully, considered. And all of this consideration has created a place which is assuredly elegant.

James Hunt's cooking suits the style of Ms Ryan's house, wearing both flair and understatement: slivers of smoked haddock and monkfish with Puy lentils and a tarragon butter sauce; beef carpaccio with parmesan and olive oil; main courses such as roast loin of lamb with a parsnip and leek purée, or wild mallard with wild mushrooms and glazed beetroot, or fillets of sole with a leek compote and roasted endive.

Puddings are sinful, and will likely make you wish you had walked a rake of miles before dinner: bread and butter pudding sharpened with a splash of whiskey; rich dark chocolate cake with chocolate sauce; creamed rice pudding. It is a very good idea indeed to have had a long walk, because here is a house where you simply should not skip the cheeseboard. Sourced from Peter Ward's shop, Country Choice, a few miles up the road in Nenagh, it is one of the very best selections of Irish farmhouse cheeses you will find in Ireland.

It makes for a smashing dinner in a smashing house, just the sort of retreat on the banks of the Shannon one craves, just the sort of food to head home to after a day's boating or walking, when you are hungry from the fresh air and mustard keen for the crack to continue.

■ OPEN:
7pm-9pm Tue-Sun
■ AVERAGE PRICE:
Dinner £26.50
House Wine from £10.50
■ CREDIT CARDS:
Visa, Access/Master

■ NOTES:
Restaurant Licence
Wheelchair Access, but not to toilet
Children – welcome, high chair
From Limerick city take the N7 to Dublin. At Birdhill take the road signposted Killaloe.
In the village of Ballina/Killaloe drive straight through – Waterman's Lodge is on the outskirts of the village on the left hand side.

McCLUSKEY'S BISTRO

Paul & Monica McCluskey
18 High Street
Waterford
Co Waterford
Tel: (051) 857766

Head Chef: Stephen Mullally

Paul McCluskey not only looks much younger than his accumulation of years, he is a chef who has always cooked like a young man, and not like someone with decades of experience in the business. Chefs usually tire as the years go by, they usually begin to repeat themselves, and to become content to mine a groove established when they were still young. Mr. McCluskey is an exception to this rule.

His cooking is enlivened, and thereby enlivening. He initiates new ideas, assimilates new fashions in cooking. His work may have many elements of classical cooking about it, but it has always held onto a simplicity and a respect for ingredients which is delightful.

He moved into this new part of town a while back, into a straightforward room which was a decisive contrast to his previous gig at the plush, patrician Waterford Castle. He seems happier here, doing something simpler, more in tune with his philosophy of using distinctive local foods – Tom Phelan's sausages with a herb mash, or a great rocket salad with Waterford's excellent Knockalara cheese, or Bannow Bay mussels with white wine and herbs – food which enjoys all the tenor and hunger of a young blade.

He is a fine fish cook, making utterly lovely cod with a Thai sauce, adapted from a Rick Stein recipe, pairing salmon and monkfish with saffron as a foil for some tagliatelle, whilst the soulful, gentle side of his work is found in fine Tunisian lamb served with couscous or organic red rice.

As befits a man who has always seemed somewhat ahead of his time, he presents creative vegetarian cooking, such as a Mediterranean bean stew with basmati rice, or linguini with tomato, spinach, salsa verde and Parmesan.

Prices are extremely good, and the wine list is similarly inexpensive, arranged according to price and with only a few bottles allowing you to push the financial boat out. Indeed, this combination of good food at good prices, with good wines and good service, shows all the experience that both Paul and Monica McCluskey have acquired over the years, and shows it being put to good use.

■ OPEN:
Noon-2.30pm, 6pm-10pm Tue-Sat
■ AVERAGE PRICE:
Lunch from £5
Dinner from £25
House Wine from £10.50
■ CREDIT CARDS:
Visa, Access/Master

■ NOTES:
Wine Licence
Recommended for Vegetarians
Wheelchair Access
Children – welcome, high chair, half portions
High Street is parallel to the Quay, near the City Square Car Park.

THE WINE VAULT

David Dennison
High Street
Waterford
Co Waterford
Tel: (051) 53444
Fax: 53444

Head Chef: Paul Brady

A friend once described the secret of David Dennison's splendid Wine Vault as resulting from the fact that "this place feels like a restaurant. During lunch, people came and went, people talked aloud, deliveries were made, phones rang, plates clattered, the espresso machine burbled, the waiter waited. A nice, well-run, how-it-should-be restaurant".

David Dennison is an enthusiast, with the ability to coax enthusiasm out of both his team, and his customers. He is not just passionate about wine, he is obsessive about it, and about matching wine with food.

His devotion means that the 'Vault is really a shrine to his love of wine and food, and it is a devotion he wants to share with you: there is no stand-offishness here, no professional distance maintained. You go into the 'Vault and you go pell-mell for a good time.

As our friend remarked, "I half expected a Fiat millecento or whatever – to draw up outside and the visiting cousins to arrive, all the men kissing each other and slapping backs, all the women arguing in the air and fat children skulking...".

But Mr. Dennison's bistro is not a place for Italian trattoria rubbish. What it does instead is imbibe the air of a European bistro, and breathe it anew in Waterford: at times in here, you feel you could be in some little place in the South of France or on the Italian border or somewhere in the Pyrenees. It is the pulse of people having a good time.

The food is simple and effective: mussels cooked the way they should be – big, juicy, garlic-rich. Fresh haddock, perfectly cooked. Oysters baked with a sauté of leek and lemon. Pan roasted barbary duck. excellent desserts such as chocolate roulade or a fine homemade ice cream.

One important tip when in the Wine Vault – aside from making sure to buy some wine from the shop to take with you – is to ask for some advice about matching wines with the food you choose. This is Mr. Dennison's ultimate aim: that his customers should hit on that magical, alchemical moment when good food and terrific wine conjoin.

■ OPEN:
12.30pm-2.30pm, 5.30pm-10.30pm Mon-Sat ('till 11pm Sat)
■ AVERAGE PRICE:
Lunch £10
Dinner from £25-£30
House Wine from £10.50
■ CREDIT CARDS:
Visa, Access/Master, Amex

■ NOTES:
Wine Licence
Wheelchair Access
Children – welcome
Recommended for Vegetarians
High Street is parallel to the Quay.
Near the City Square Car Park.

CROOKEDWOOD HOUSE

Noel & Julie Kenny
Crookedwood
Mullingar
Co Westmeath
Tel: (044) 73165
Fax: 72166

Head Chef: Noel Kenny

The challenge which faces every serious, seriously-minded chef who works in Ireland is that of stating and demonstrating a true regional cuisine.

And it is the challenge of finding, and creating, the tastes of Westmeath, which is the imprimatur hungrily seized upon by Noel Kenny, the chef-proprietor of Crookedwood House, just outside the little hamlet of that name.

Crookedwood is a fine old pile, and a house to which Noel Kenny has brought considerable honour thanks to his considered, powerful style of cooking.

He loves to work with the foods of the area, which he manipulates in alliance with the multitude of vegetables and herbs which he grows himself. Breast of wild duck is oozingly savoury and perfectly counterpointed by a port and onion marmalade, or the same duck may be paired with venison. This original pairing of ingredients is a game Mr Kenny loves to play, even down to his own original surf 'n' turf where he parcels up salmon in filo pastry and teams it with a honey glazed pork.

The Hunter's plate finds this love of admixture again, with venison, quail and pigeon in a red wine and game jus, whilst local lamb has the elegant idea of a kohlrabi purée. The extraordinary beef which Mr Kenny sources from Tormey's, of Mullingar, may be stuffed with wild mushrooms, or used with duck livers. But whatever the ideas played out on the plate, one is always struck by the fact that Mr Kenny's work is devoted to its region, to the flavours of the foods of Westmeath, to those tastes with their rich heritage of small-scale agriculture and careful animal husbandry.

It is important to state the singularity of the cooking in Crookedwood, for much as we have tended in the past to overlook Westmeath as someplace to stop and dally and explore, we have certainly overlooked the idea that it might have its own style of cooking. But, of course, it has that style, a style which echoes the place itself: generous, patiently expressive, country cooking, in the heart of the country.

■ OPEN:
7pm-10pm Tue-Sat, 12.30pm-2.30pm Sun

■ AVERAGE PRICE:
Sunday Lunch £13.50
Dinner from £21
House Wine from £11.50

■ CREDIT CARDS:
Visa, Access/Master, Amex, Diners

■ NOTES:
Restaurant Licence
No Wheelchair Access, but happy to help
Children – welcome if well behaved, high chair, half portions and children's favourites
Coming from Dublin, take the 3rd exit off Mullingar by-pass, signed for Castlepollard. Drive to Crookedwood village. Turn right at Wood Pub, then 1 1/2 miles further along you will see the house.

THE LEFT BANK BISTRO

Mary McCullagh & Annie McNamara
Bastion Street
Athlone
Co Westmeath
Tel: (0902) 94446 Fax: 94446

Head Chef: Annie McNamara

There is something rather lovely about Annie McNamara and Mary McCullagh's Left Bank Bistro. In a town which offers little that is aesthetically pleasing, this little trove of rooms is in the old part of Athlone, on the Connaught side of the Shannon, an entrancing mix of narrow, winding streets and some funky, left-field shops.

The funky left-field is where Annie and Mary's cooking comes from. Ms McNamara is Australian by birth, and the foods of the Pacific Rim are the ones which attract her skills: Thai spiced chicken breast on egg noodles in coconut milk, chilli, lemon grass and coriander; spicy black bean burrito with melted cheese; fried potato skins with a tomato and chilli dipping sauce; tiger prawns in warm garlic and piri piri.

This is lovely cooking, modern but not at all self-conscious, confident and expert, and where Annie and Mary have also sounded a departure for the Midlands is in serving the food in a relaxed, enjoyable, nouveau pauvre building, a space which is organised in just the right way to set the tone of the place.

The blackboard announces the day's specials, there is a counter behind which the wine is stored, and the old pine and bare boards nature of the room is perfectly judged which, along with the good cooking, explains the success the girls have enjoyed ever since they opened up here.

And, though you might sometimes question the wisdom of ordering fish in the centre of the country, here is a restaurant where you can do so with confidence: char-grilled squid with chillis and coriander; fillet of brill with garlic roasted pinenuts; barbecued Atlantic salmon with lime and dill. At each point, with each dish, Annie likes to throw in an unconventional, surprising gesture, and little secret touches.

Service, like everything else around here, is charming, gracious, in tune with the beat of a restaurant that is cool, calm, collected. There is a short wine list which is fairly priced but somewhat uninspiring. Overall, however, this is the right restaurant in the right place at the right time.

■ OPEN:
10.30am-6pm Mon-Sat, 6pm-9pm Thur-Sat (open 10.30am-10pm Mon-Sat summer months)

■ AVERAGE PRICE:
Lunch £5.50
Dinner £15-£20
House Wine from £9.95

■ CREDIT CARDS:
Visa, Access/Master

■ NOTES:
Wine Licence
Wheelchair Access, but not to toilets
Children – welcome
Located in the old part of Athlone, on Connaught side of Shannon river, behind

WINEPORT RESTAURANT

Ray Byrne & Jane English
Glasson, Athlone, Co Westmeath
Tel: (0902) 85466 Fax: 85471
e-mail: wineport@iol.ie

Head Chef: Noel Ryan

A simple, four-square room in wood, with big windows from which we can spy out across the glinting waters, Ray Byrne and Jane English's Wineport is a terrific space.

Perfectly, romantically lit by snaky, fin-de-siecle lamps and candles, there is a cosy entrance lounge with a fire blazing in front of comfy couches, a lovely statement of simplicity. Within its locality, Ray and Jane's restaurant is something of a phenomenon. Business is so good, they have recently had to build the new Chart Room, which is used for functions and parties.

Its success is built on the fact that folk come because the food in Wineport is real food: simple, well-conceived, with good, true tastes, the sort of dishes that sing loud and long to a good appetite: three bean soup with coriander; baked scallops in filo; fillets of trout with tarragon; fusilli with Mediterranean vegetables, mixed nuts and goat's cheese.

The carte might offer spicy chicken wings with a rhubarb and yogurt dip; local smoked salmon and eel; rack of lamb with tomato and oregano sauce; chicken stuffed with a leek mousse; the brilliant, inimitable Westmeath beef with a brandy and Glasson mushroom sauce.

Sunday lunch, which may be the best time to come here, offers delights such as butterbean dumplings in tomato sauce with melted mozzarella; potato cakes spiked with shallots served with an apple marmalade; confit of duck with a rich fruit sauce, chicken and mushroom kebabs with savoury rice. Delightful cooking, designed for the entire family to enjoy.

But the dynamic change which Wineport represents is a social one, and lies with their ability to make a restaurant someplace truly democratic: appealing to young, old and in-betweenies, appealing to golfers and boaty types, appealing to couples escaping the babies for a few hours and footloose and fancy-free twenty-somethings.

And, having attracted these disparate sorts out here to the water, Wineport delivers a good time. Their collusion of effects – the ambience, the friendliness, the keenly-priced wines which you choose from out of the recess yourself, the tasty food – is irresistible. In an efficient, unselfconscious way, they are changing the way in which people use, and enjoy, restaurants.

■ OPEN:
5pm-10pm Mon-Sun, 12.30pm-3.30pm Sun

■ AVERAGE PRICE:
Sunday Lunch £13.95. Dinner £20
House Wine from £10.50

■ CREDIT CARDS:
Visa, Access/Master, Amex

■ NOTES:
Restaurant Licence
Full Wheelchair Access
Children – welcome, high chair, menus
Take exit 4 on Athlone relief road, 2 miles out is a very sharp bend which is actually a village called Ballykeeran. Follow signs from the Dog & Duck in Ballykeeran.

AVOCA HANDWEAVERS

The Pratt Family
Kilmacanogue, Bray, Co Wicklow
Tel: (01) 286 7466 Fax: 286 2367

Head Chef: Joanna Hill

The Avoca Handweavers restaurant is a phenomenon.

It is no more than a great big dining space, serviced by a single counter, which is appended to a shop where they sell crafts, fashions and foods. And, for a phenomenally large number of days each year, it serves food of a phenomenally high standard to phenomenally large numbers of people.

How do they do it?

Well, for one thing, they have a team of smart young women in charge, whose command and control of their work is extraordinary. Leylie Hayes directs matters, Joanna Hill is the talented head chef, and around them works a team who bristle with ideas, and who all share a common vision of good food at good prices in a good place as being an ideal they must achieve every day.

This is what counts. What they do at Avoca is cooking, not catering. They never slide into complacency. They never compromise on the quality of ingredients. They never take short cuts, making all the foods from scratch all the time.

Two things, then, are their signature. The first is that the cooking is just delicious. The piperade and goat's cheese tart is practically a modern Irish classic. The chicken Italian served with pasta and a mixed leaf salad is scrummy with yummy flavours. The soups – celery and Cashel Blue cheese; potato and fennel; sweet tomato and pesto; rich minestrone with croIutons and parmesan – are an index of the soup-maker's art.

Their salads are distinguished by freshness, and by intelligent pairing of ingredients with diverse dressings. Their cooked meats are placed into the service of sandwiches – crispy baguette with home-baked ham and a ripe tomato chutney; chicken with roasted pepper mayonnaise and Parmesan on tomato foccaccia – and their own brown bread is sweet as cake.

And their cakes are as sweet as the brown bread: chocolate fudge cake; Avoca apple tart; baked cheesecake; meringue roulade with fruit; citrus tart.

People travel from far and wide to enjoy the cooking at Avoca, and it is an institution which shines like a beacon. To be able to create so much satisfaction and happiness amongst so many people is a mighty feat, and something Ms Hill and Ms Hayes and the Pratt family – who own Avoca – should be very proud of.

■ OPEN:
9.30pm-5.30pm Mon-Sun

■ AVERAGE PRICE:
Lunch £8-£14. House Wine from £8.95

■ CREDIT CARDS:
Visa, Access/Master, Amex, Diners

■ NOTES:
Wine Licence
Full Wheelchair Access
Children – welcome, high chair
On the N11 main Dublin/Wexford Road, 3 miles beyond the Bray exit and 500 yards before Kilmacanogue village.

THE OLD RECTORY COUNTRY HOUSE

Paul & Linda Saunders
Wicklow, Co Wicklow
Tel: (0404) 67048 Fax: 69181
e-mail: oldrec@indigo.ie

Head Chef: Linda Saunders

Pastel pink-painted and petite, Paul and Linda Saunders' Old Rectory is a vital and essential asset to the town and the County of Wicklow.

It is a place which, in many ways, directly reflects the character of Mrs Saunders herself: composed, complex, reserved, determined, it is a house and restaurant which acts as a showcase for Mrs Saunders' involved, intricate cooking, a cuisine which, itself, almost acts as a showcase for the strengths and delights of the county of Wicklow itself.

She uses superb organic ingredients, grown locally, which explains firstly why her food always has a vibrancy and freshness about it, reflecting the sunshiney, youthful nature of the Wicklow hills.

Then, to this, she brings a high degree of invention and expressiveness – and an astute and intellectually broad understanding for the architecture of taste – which few other country house cooks can match.

Indeed, the sense of complex and compatible flavouring in her food is reminiscent of the structure of a perfume, for she seems to build tastes in a way which is almost vertical, with alluring scents and involved taste structures to be enjoyed both in the main dishes themselves and in their compatriot sauces.

A warm terrine of salmon and sea trout will, then, swim along with a green herb sauce, whilst parsnips will pair off with red beans for a soup, and the elegant ruddiness of a carrot and cucumber tart will have the warm spice of marjoram underpinning it. Details echo the principal theme in a way which is almost musical.

Typically, Mrs Saunders takes her skills to the far outreaches of creativity, composing dinner menus to arrive at compatible complexity and, to celebrate the Wicklow Flower Festival, she cooks a daring ten course Floral Dinner: kale flower purses in filo; gazpacho ropjo with iced borrage blossoms; roast quail stuffed with apple, pine nut and sage flowers, a joyful jamboree of tastes which is delightfully endless.

This is very intriguing cooking, and quite unique, its sense of balance and order very feminine and organic.

■ **OPEN:**
8pm Mon-Sun

■ **AVERAGE PRICE:**
Dinner from £28.50
House Wine from £13

■ **CREDIT CARDS:**
Visa, Access/Master, Amex, Diners

■ **NOTES:**
Wine Licence
No Wheelchair Access
Children – welcome if well behaved, high chair, children's gourmet menu @ £14.25 available on request, otherwise dishes priced as ordered
From Dublin take the N11 to Rathnew, then R750 to Wicklow town. The entrance to the house is on the left, 100 yards after the Jet Garage.

TINAKILLY COUNTRY HOUSE AND RESTAURANT

William & Bee Power
Rathnew, Co Wicklow
Tel: (0404) 67274 Fax: 67806

Head Chef: John Moloney

If one could fairly say that it is ambition which sets Tinakilly apart from other hotels – an ambition which makes them try harder, which makes them strive to achieve more, which continually puts pressure on themselves to improve – then one has to say that nowhere throughout this fine hotel is this more in evidence than in the kitchen.

John Moloney's cooking is mightily impressive, and it has the great – and necessary – virtue of being impressive to one and all.

If you are a conservative chap who enjoys the sweet, satisfying and simple flavours of roasted meats and poached fish, then you will be comforted and delighted by Mr Moloney's work: escalopes of monkfish with a feuillete of winter vegetables and a beurre blanc; roast pheasant with a celeriac mash; loin of lamb with a potato and leek galette, fine cooking which is expertly administered.

If, on the other hand, you are a cool class of fellow who wants to find something closer to the cutting edge, then you will find it here also; wild mushroom tart with a sun-dried tomato dressing; fresh scallops on a salad of orange and tomato with a rocket pesto; loin of lamb with a caper mash.

This is an impressive double act for a restaurant to pull off, especially an hotel restaurant which faces extra demands. "We strive to combine the best of country house cooking with an original and modern approach..." says Mr Moloney, and it is neither a wistful nor an idle boast. \he can do it.

Away from the standard menus, they can orchestrate the contents of their gourmet dinners as smartly as Busby Berkeley. A fresh lobster salad with a raspberry vinaigrette has the shellfish splayed around the edge of a bed of salad leaves. This rich sternness is followed by the killer punch that is a warm chicken mousse, slightly gelatinous in texture, blue cheese oozing from the centre, the dish is suffused with the tastes of chicken, cheese and sweet butter. Well-balanced, true-flavoured, sassy, excellent cooking.

Where others try to please everyone and end up by pleasing no one, at Tinakilly they manage the difficult act of cooking food which is guest-friendly, and yet creative enough to draw in the curious food lover. That is no mean feat.

■ **OPEN:**
12.30pm-2pm Mon-Sun, 7.30pm-9pm Mon-Sat, 7.30pm-8.30pm Sun
■ **AVERAGE PRICE:**
Lunch £18.50. Dinner £32
House Wine from £12
■ **CREDIT CARDS:**
Visa, Access/Master, Amex, Diners

■ **NOTES:**
Hotel Bar Licence
Full Wheelchair Access
Children – welcome, high chair
Tinakilly is 500m from Rathnew on the R750 for Wicklow.

northern ireland

DEANE'S

Michael Deane
Howard Street
Belfast
Co Antrim
Tel: (01232)

Head chef: Michael Deane

Michael Deane has had perhaps the slowest gestation period of any of the trail-blazing cooks from the North, but it is clear now that his period of steady work at Deane's, in Helen's Bay, has allowed him to develop a style, and a confidence, which means that he has found the perfect mechanisms by which to express himself.

He loves to take things apart, and then to rebuild classic dishes in his own manner. This is fun work, but unless the dish can be built back to total completeness, it won't wash.

So, it is doubly satisfying then, that his revision of a classic salad niçoise, to accompany a stunningly achieved dish of brandade de morue, will separate out all the ingredients of the salad and then reconfigure them with their compatible taste elements perfectly re-unified. Terrific fun, and terrifically successful.

He loves to renovate traditional things like risotto also, making the dish with pearl barley, serving it with some pigeon and some ethereal foie gras, and then sending the dish into the heavens with the use of a perfectly matched lemon oil.

This is mature cooking, by a chef who has found that his style works best when he produces dishes which balance his love of innovation with a true understanding of what the innovation can achieve in terms of taste. There are no gratuitous touches, no cheffy conceit. The cooking works.

Having mastered the challenge of developing a mature style, Michael Deane now faces the big challenge as he moves his restaurant into Belfast, to a corner building on Howard Street in the centre of the city.

There would appear to be a parallel here with Derry Clarke, of Dublin's L'Ecrivain, another chef who, at roughly the same age as Mr Deane, moved premises, moved up a gear, and has been on a roll ever since. Michael Deane is moving at just the right time.

The more formal cooking of Deane's in Helen's Bay will continue upstairs, whilst downstairs will see a more informal space for inexpensive eating. Wine lists will be much more extensive, and the good folk of Belfast will wish that all the staff will be as brilliant at their job as Mark Boyd, Mr Deane's waiter, who is a peerless performer.

■ **OPEN:**
Restaurant: 12.30pm-7.30pm Tue-Sat;
Brasserie: noon-midnight Mon-Sat

■ **AVERAGE PRICE:**
Restaurant Lunch £15-£20
Restaurant Dinner £25-£30
Brasserie Lunch & Dinner £5-£20

■ **CREDIT CARDS:**
Visa, Access/Master, Amex, Diners

■ **NOTES:**
Wine Licence
Wheelchair Access to Brasserie
Children – welcome in Brasserie
Near the City Hall in Beflast city centre.

NICK'S WAREHOUSE

Nick & Kathy Price
35-39 Hill Street, Belfast BT1 2LB
Tel: (01232) 439690 Fax: 230514

Head Chef: Nick Price

It's difficult to understand why the media has not latched on to Nick Price in the same way it has made stars out of some of his Northern colleagues.

He is a splendidly funny man, with an inimitable way with words, as he demonstrates with both his menus and his wine lists. Indeed, for sheer amusement – and accuracy – this man leaves every other wine list compiler in the country standing. He could be the Oz Clarke of Belfast, if he got the break, and maybe even the new Graham Kerr of the telly.

His cooking, likewise, is light-hearted and amused with itself. He cooks seriously, but without ponderousness or portentiousness, so that you understand that enjoying his food is more important than analysing which contemporary culinary point he has newly staked out.

But stake them out he does. Something delicious and smart like a marinated brie and oven-dried tomato salad is the sort of vogueish dish you might expect from Alastair Little or somesuch, and Mr Price renders it deliciously. He can do a twist on the repertoire of black pudding dishes, serving his with red wine lentils and roast shallots, whilst a salad of duck confit with avocado and sweet pepper salsa again shows his enjoyment of assimilating new ideas, taking new themes and making them his own with instinctive and imaginative flourishes of flavour and finesse.

Irrespective of what he cooks, Mr Price's food always returns home to succulence and spoonsomeness. A vegetarian dish such as a casserole of barley and haricot beans with mushrooms, peppers and tomatoes is subtle and perfectly balanced, a tempura of lemon sole is perfectly cooked and super-charged by a sweet chilli and ginger sauce. He can cook things like lamb chops with garlic and rocket butter as if he was born to it.

In fact, Nick Price almost makes the whole thing seem easy. He doe not seem to have much concern for the fact that he is one of the most important restaurateurs in the North, and has been so for two decades. He doesn't see himself as a trailblazer in terms of creating brilliant restaurant spaces in unlikely places, but he is vitally important because he has done this. He and Kathy Price are a treasure of the city, a treasure that should not be missed.

■ **OPEN:**
Noon-3pm wine bar; noon-2.30pm restaurant, 6pm-9pm winebar & restaurant Mon-Fri, 6pm-11pm Sat. Wine bar open for coffee and drinks 11.30am-5pm Mon, 11.30am-11pm Tue-Fri

■ **AVERAGE PRICE:**
Lunch £2.75-£5.50 wine bar
£19 restaurant
Dinner from £17.95-£19.95

■ **CREDIT CARDS:**
Visa, Access/Master, Amex, Diners

■ **NOTES:**
Full Pub Licence. Wheelchair Access
Children – welcome in restaurant only
In the centre of Belfast.

ROSCOFF ✪

Paul & Jeanne Rankin
7 Lesley House
Shaftesbury Square, Belfast BT2
Tel: (01232) 331532 Fax: 312093

It is worth stating a simple fact about Paul and Jeanne Rankin's Roscoff restaurant, given that their rise to pre-eminence in the media seems, nowadays, to attract little other than brickbats from locals.

Roscoff is the restaurant which revolutionised restaurant cooking and eating in the North, and it remains a benchmark of achievement for restaurateurs in Ireland.

Its combination of originality, creativity and superb service was years ahead of its competitors, and Northerners not only took to it like ducks to water, they very quickly took it for granted.

Add in a dose of healthy begrudgery, and suddenly everyone is running around saying "It's not as good as it used to be!".

This is ignorant bunkum. It is true that Roscoff is not as dynamic and driven a restaurant when Mr Rankin is away from the stove, but it even then can outpace almost everywhere else for style and accomplishment. Indeed, Paul Rankin has been unlucky in never finding a lieutenant who has stayed with him over the years, and who might have helped to keep things on a more even keel. Instead, his kitchen staff have themselves gone off to achieve great things, inspired by his example and success.

And, truly, inspiration is what Roscoff is all about. On song, on form, it is a mighty, perfect thing, a fluid and brilliant confirmation of all the romance and mystique which a restaurant can achieve.

Despite the pressures of the media, Mr Rankin's work continues to be obsessively progressive. He will make a gratin of squid ink pasta and prawns and tie up the sea-salty squid and sweet shellfish flavours into an explosive knot of taste.

But, like the dramatic cook he is, he understands the need for tension to be followed by release, so some squab on mustard greens with shallots and chives shows another side of his work: relaxed, tender tastes which satisfy profoundly. He gets enjoyment out of the classics – wild trout with a perfect dill hollandaise; goat's cheese croquettes on rocket; chicken with a saffron mash; fantastic caramel crème brûlée with a mighty rhubarb compote – food which, in combination with brilliant service and this coolest of cool rooms, is irresistible.

Roscoff remains an inspirational restaurant, and a place of inspired, unique, cooking.

■ OPEN:
12.30pm-2.15pm Mon-Fri, 6.30pm-10.15pm Mon-Sat

■ AVERAGE PRICE:
Lunch £16.50
Dinner from £28.95
House Wine from £11.95

■ CREDIT CARDS:
Visa, Access/Master, Amex, Diners

■ NOTES:
Full Licence
Wheelchair Access
Children – welcome, high chair
Top of Great Victoria Street in city centre.

THE SUN KEE

Edmund Lau
28 Donegal Pass
Belfast BT7
Tel: (01232) 312016

Head Chef: Edmund Lau

Imagine a little Chinese restaurant where the owners remember who you are when you walk through the door, and where they greet you with a bright smile and a "Hello!".

A place where they listen painstakingly to awkward orders, and accommodate the sort of requests which, in other Chinese restaurants, are met with a polite, but firm, "Not possible". A Chinese restaurant where they open the bottles of wine you have bought yourself, and don't expect you to soldier through on Liebfraumilch and classless claret.

Imagine, finally, a Chinese eating house where the food is gloriously real and true tasting: nervy, exciting, spicy and delicious, a million miles from the hotch-potch of Hong-Kong-meets-Cantonese which most Chinese restaurants trade in.

You don't need to imagine this little Chinese restaurant. It exists. It's called The Sun Kee. It's run by Edmund Lau, in Belfast, on Donegal Pass.

The Sun Kee dispels with the idea that Chinese cooking, for Irish tastes, cannot be truly authentic, for this is real food and it enjoys the glorious pairing of tastes which is the great invention of Chinese cooking.

The monkfish with char siu is a thrill. Served in a hot-pot dish, it has little clusters of deep-fried fish fighting it out with thin slices of the delectable char siu. By teaming it with the monkfish, the two propel each other into the taste stratosphere. The beef flank hotpot demonstrates a rusticity we rarely find in the bourgeois Chinese restaurants, slow cooking bringing a tender texture to the potatoes and the turnips which are the bedfellows of the beef. Duck stuffed with prawns is slithery, gloopy and squidgy, a wobbly glaze of egg white forming a transparent film over the slices of duck and the prawn paste.

The assorted gaggle of folk whom we have brought to the restaurant on subsequent visits, bods and sods of all sorts and from all sorts of culinary backgrounds, have unanimously praised it as the finest Chinese cooking they have eaten.

But there is even more to admire about the Sun Kee than the smashing food. It is terrifically cheap, almost everyone else eating in the restaurant is a member of Belfast's Chinese community, the waiters bill and coo and, indeed, even kiss your baby. You won't be able to resist it.

■ OPEN:
5pm-1am Mon-Thur
5pm-11.30pm Sat
5pm-1am Sun.

■ AVERAGE PRICE:
Dinner from £12

■ CREDIT CARDS:
No credit cards.

■ NOTES:
No Licence.
Bring your own wine
Wheelchair Access
Children – welcome, high chair
Beside the police station on Donegal Pass.

RAMORE RESTAURANT

George & Jane McAlpin
The Harbour, Portrush
Co Antrim, BT56 8BN
Tel: (01265) 824313

Head Chef: George McAlpin

It has been the most marvellous fun, not to mention the most delicious fun, to see how The Ramore has altered its character over the last couple of years, and become a simpler, more successful, more democratic and much funkier place to eat.

The re-invention began with the creation of a more informal dining space, the kitchen fully open to view and a set of bar chairs at the counter.

The paraphernalia of a working kitchen – the batallions of knives and brigades of whisks, the knots of garlic, the green-hued bottles of olive oil, the spattered cookery texts, are all on happy exhibition along with their white-clad employers, who intersect with one another with the sure-footedness of dancers. It's a charming entertainment, as you sip aperitifs and nibble bread, but when the food arrives, it is quickly heads-down to see what is on the plate.

For in parallel with the stylistic renovation, George McAlpin's cooking has shifted its concentration away from a French style, and has brought on board the lighter and more appropriate influences of the Pacific Rim.

Thus, whilst we find the signatures of foreign influence dotted throughout the dishes – smashing tempura prawns with diced peppers under a trio of Mexican tostados; tagliatelle with a just-right Roquefort sauce; char-grilled chicken with sun-dried tomatoes for annotation – it is almost as much fun to stick with George's revisions of classic dishes, for they reveal a great sense of humour and creativity.

You can eat prawn cocktail, and then steak and chips with fried onion rings in here, and it will be a belter of a meal: the cocktail expertly made with perfect ingredients, the steak served with onion rings so crisp and light they could be called tempura, the chips pure magic. Some monkfish with utterly splendid local scallops, lightly coated in breadcrumbs, will have their saline succulence perfectly captured by quick frying, a mastery of fish cookery.

Chicken and duck liver parfait has a column of melba toast stored high in the style of railway sleepers, whilst with traditional fish 'n' chips, exquisitely fresh fish is balanced atop a tower of perfect chips in a dazzling architectural tumbril.

The staff are super-duper, the wine list short and clever – house wines are very good here – and the whole organisation devoted to delivering the best of the best of times.

■ **OPEN:**
6.30pm-10.30pm Tue-Sat
■ **AVERAGE PRICE:**
Dinner from £22.50
House Wine from £8.50
■ **CREDIT CARDS:**
Visa, Access/Master

■ **NOTES:**
Full Pub Licence
Wheelchair Access, but not to toilets
Children – welcome until 9pm
On the harbour at Portrush.

SHANKS ✪

Robbie & Shirley Millar
The Blackwood
150 Crawfordsburn Road
Clandeboye, Bangor, Co Down
Tel: (01247) 853313 Fax: 853785

Head Chef: Robbie Millar

You could argue long into the night about the ways in which Robbie Millar's cooking has changed in the last year or so. You might wonder whether the classical element in his background is now asserting pre-eminence over the iconoclastic notes which have been a trademark, but the unavoidable conclusion one will draw is that his food is gloriously satisfying, and fun, and devoted to giving pleasure. What is more, he is a chef at the peak of his powers.

His classical side appears to be on the ascendant – you could have a dinner of baked goat's cheese tart, grilled loin of lamb, maybe a daube of beef with a potato and Parmesan ravioli, and then fresh lemon tart, or his remarkable chocolate tart – and the different elements will be as perfectly stated as one could hope for, exactingly correct, meticulous.

But the iconoclast still likes to have fun – working variations on crostini combinations, such as asparagus, mushrooms, cheese and truffle oil, by shifting the cheese to ruffles of tete de moine and adding in some grilled fennel – or making scallion rice cakes as a partner for grilled duck breast and completing the Oriental note by making a hoi sin sauce.

But whatever the outcome of this dialogue between the old and the new, Mr Millar's food remains focused on deliciousness, simple and true. You can eat scallops here – peppered, with delicious creamed orzo and a scarf of leeks topped with a shiitake mushroom hat – and they are better than anyone else's, the sweetness stunningly seared into the little coins of shellfish. Any debate about the history of a dish of lamb and beans goes out the window when the meld of sweet meat and perfect beans arrives, its subtle flavours abetted by jade green spinach and a garlic and parsley jus.

What impresses with this cooking is its confidence and its understanding of the symmetry of tastes which can work together to make a dish perfect. Judgement, in other words. Knowing when enough is enough.

Desserts show the same fluent, parade of flavour: to-die-for warm chocolate tart with vanilla ice cream; subtle lemongrass syrup and coconut ice cream with tropical fruits.

The dining rooms in Shanks are restrained and elegant places, service is fabulous, the wine list brilliant, and value for money is remarkable.

■ OPEN:
12.30pm-2.30pm Tue-Fri
7pm-10pm Tue-Sat, 12.30pm-2pm Sun
■ AVERAGE PRICE:
Lunch £12.95-£16.95. Dinner £28.50
■ CREDIT CARDS:
Visa, Access/Master, Amex

■ NOTES:
Full Pub Licence
Wheelchair Access
Children – welcome, high chair, special menu
Situated in the Blackwood Golf Centre.

THE YELLOW DOOR

Roisin Hendron & Simon Dougan
Gilford, nr Banbridge, Co Down
Tel: (01762) 831543

Head Chef: Simon Dougan

The Yellow Door is a restaurant distinguished by an admirable application, an admirable determination to do things properly.

You don't think this when you first get a glimpse of it, however. Tucked tight into the side of the road, on a hill, opposite a small housing estate, it looks like a mix of shebeen-meets-steak-house.

You walk into a small reception area, a mix of sofas and comfy chairs, and the first hint that you are someplace serious is the presence of a pair of glass cabinets which are strewn with much-leafed cookery books. Reassuring.

The menus promise intriguing cooking - Moroccan spiced fillet of lamb with couscous and roast vegetables; fresh pasta with smoked chicken and a fresh herb pesto; cannon of pork with cabbage and bacon and a parsley cream sauce; supreme of chicken with Thai fried rice - and the kitchen does not dissipate that promise.

Roisin Hendron and her team are serious, and it shows in the attention to detail. A starter of salmon and leek tart served with dressed salad leaves has a perfect pastry – crumbly, buttery, rich – which perfectly conjoins with the eggy collation of salmon and leeks. The salad was lightly dressed, refreshing.

Fresh pasta with smoked chicken and a fresh herb pesto scores on all points; the tagliatelle excellent, the smoked chicken a presence in the dish rather than an overpowering element, the pesto bristling with freshness.

Roast Irish lamb with colcannon and a rich lamb jus is right on the money, a trio of cutlets arranged around a tower of colcannon, with a jus that had been reduced to perfection: syrupy, full of flavour, neither too strong nor too viscous.

Grilled fillet of hake is served on top of some sautéed greens and diced mange tout, the firm flesh of the twin fillets counterpointed by a dill butter sauce which is again absolutely spot on.

The homemade ice creams are superb, the half dozen flavours including one of the most refreshing mint ices possible. Even better is a dish of profiteroles served with a hot fudge sauce. The little orbs of choux pastry cloaked in chocolate just melt in the mouth, whilst the sauce was seriously sinful. The Yellow Door is a vital spark of inspiration in an area denuded of good cooking.

OPEN:
Noon-3pm, 6.30pm-10.30pm Tue-Fri, 6.30pm-10.30pm Sat, noon-4pm Sun

■ AVERAGE PRICE:
Lunch £12.95. Dinner from £20-£25
House Wine from £10

■ CREDIT CARDS:
Visa, Access/Master, Amex, Diners

■ NOTES:
Full Licence
Wheelchair Access
Children – welcome, especially for Sunday lunch, high chair
On the road between Portadown and Banbridge.

a-z INDEX

INDEX

g

h

i

j

k

l

m

n

o

p

q

r

s

t

v

w

y

OTHER TITLES FROM ESTRAGON PRESS

WRITTEN BY
JOHN & SALLY McKENNA

THE BRIDGESTONE IRISH FOOD GUIDE

THE BRIDGESTONE VEGETARIAN GUIDE TO IRELAND

THE BRIDGESTONE DUBLIN FOOD GUIDE

THE BRIDGESTONE 100 BEST SERIES:

THE BRIDGESTONE 100 BEST PLACES TO STAY IN IRELAND

THE BRIDGESTONE TITLES ARE AVAILABLE FROM ALL GOOD BOOK SHOPS